ROLLING STONE VISITS

Saturday Night Live

*EDITED
BY
MARIANNE
PARTRIDGE*

*DESIGNED
BY
VINCENT
WINTER*

A ROLLING STONE PRESS BOOK
DOLPHIN BOOKS · DOUBLEDAY & COMPANY, INC.
GARDEN CITY, NEW YORK · 1979

Dolphin Books
Doubleday & Company, Inc.
ISBN: 0-385-15674-x
Library of Congress Catalog Card Number 79-5123

A special thanks to Lorne Michaels and the staff of
Saturday Night Live, *particularly the writers, portions of
whose scripts appear in the pages of this book. The following
articles previously appeared in* Rolling Stone: *"First
Season" (July 15, 1976); "Bill Murray" (April 20,
1978); "John Belushi" (August 10, 1978); "Gilda
Radner" (November 2, 1978); "Dan Aykroyd" (February
22, 1979); and "Blues Brothers" (February 22, 1979).
Copyright © 1976, 1978, 1979 by Straight Arrow
Publishers, Inc. We would like to thank NBC and its staff
for their cooperation in the making of this book.*

This book is dedicated to all the people at *Rolling
Stone.* Thanks for everything.

ROLLING STONE VISITS SATURDAY NIGHT LIVE

Editor : MARIANNE PARTRIDGE
Art Director : VINCENT WINTER
Consulting Editor : TIMOTHY WHITE
Photo Editor : LISBET NILSON
Editorial Production : MARTINE WINTER
Art Assistance : PATRICK CAVANAUGH, JEFF DORMAN,
ANN POMEROY, TIM REITZ, VINCENT ROMANO,
AUDREY SHACHNOW, LARRY WHITE, STEVE
ZACHARIUS
Editorial Assistance : STANLEY COHEN, MALU HALASA,
DEBBIE HURST, MARY MACDONALD, WILLIAM OEI, JERI SIMON

ROLLING STONE PRESS
Director : SARAH LAZIN

ROLLING STONE VISITS

Saturday Night Live

THE Contents

In the Green Room between dress & air: Lorne Michaels directs last-minute decisions on what goes in, what comes out; the Rolling Stones, guests, at left.

JEAN C. PIGOZZI

AN
Introduction

BY
BUCK HENRY

HERE'S THE PROBLEM. I PERsonally have never thought that they were very funny. What they have engaged, by doing whatever it is that they do, is not so much my admiration as my sympathy. Just hang around them for a while and you'll see what I mean. Take a close look at them as individuals. If you can stand it.

Belushi? A masterpiece of physiological debris. Everything in excess with the exception of simple human dignity.

Gilda Radner? Did she invent the word "neurotic?" No. But she crystallized it.

Laraine Newman? Hopelessly, helplessly, indecently thin. Thinness that virtually gives the finger to any normal person's idea of physical, hence mental, health.

Bill Murray? No one's home. It's a shell, a husk, an empty room populated by only the voices of those pathetic characters that are invented out of some residual psychic desperation.

Jane Curtin? Pretty? Not when you've seen her face twisted by some unaccountable existential agony as she sits alone, so alone, waiting for the little red light on the top of the camera to go on. The smile that *you* see? That's the smile of a breaking heart.

Garrett Morris? His own personal racial burden will never be lightened by an all too consuming interest in women's clothes.

Dan Aykroyd? I did not believe in extraterrestrial life until I met this thing. I had never come face to face with a mutant. In short—I had never stared into the face of hell.

And, of course, what was his name—Chevy. Chevy Chase? Well—let's face it—cuteness is its own worst enemy.

What can one say about a producer—in this case, one named Lorne Michaels—who persisted in bringing all of these rejects together and encouraged them to trample, week after week, on everything and everybody that Americans respect and revere. To be Canadian is not an excuse. But one must suppose that, when the final cue card is turned over, he will have a higher network to answer to.

And the others. Dozens of them. The directors, the writers, the filmmakers, the scores of technicians who make it possible for the abovementioned *chronological* adults to empty their personal garbage bins into the eyes and ears of millions of Americans on a commercially sustained basis. What possible excuse can be found for them?

I am not the one to answer that question. Because, in spite of what I have said, I have managed to reach deep within myself and, reaching, have found, ultimately, a deeper understanding. I think I *know* them. John, Gilda, Laraine, Bill, Jane, Garrett, Dan, Chevy. Even Lorne. I think I know them. I may even love them. Perhaps it's because I relate to the *possibility* of goodness. Or perhaps it's because I have slept with every one of them.

JODY CARAVAGLIA

SOME
Background

BY TIMOTHY WHITE

the Marx Brothers. Hell, he'd probably agree.

— CHEVY CHASE, *humorist*

I'm sorry but I'm not familiar with Mr. Chase or the Saturday Night Live *program.*

— S.J. PERELMAN, *humorist*

When I was a boy, my father used to read S.J. Perelman to me. I grew up admiring his ability to pinpoint the things that irk everyone. His humor had a warmth, yet it cut through the bullcrap. Much of the material on Saturday Night *was part of a natural progression from things like Perelman's prose and his work with*

SINCE ITS INCEPTION IN 1975, *Saturday Night Live* has had a tremendous impact on our lives. Not only have thirty million people tailored their weekend socializing to fit the show's 11:30 to 1:00 schedule, but their perception of what television can be has been altered as well.

ROLLING STONE has taken a particular interest in viewing, reviewing, and chronicling the breakthroughs in television comedy over the last ten years. Most notable was David Felton's masterful "Jive Times," a two-part 1974 article on the work of Lily Tomlin and Richard Pryor, in which Felton explored these gifted performers' pitched battles with traditional television. *Saturday Night Live* first aired a year later and from the start I had a lot of stimulating conversations about the show with David, Associate Editor Charles M. Young, and friends like comedy writer "Miami" Mitch Glazer (who became an invaluable help in realizing this book). These talks inevitably concluded with the enthusiastic pronouncement that here was one of the best comedy series on the tube since the days of *Your Show of Shows* and *The Ernie Kovacs Show.*

"*Saturday Night Live*'s contribution to television has a lot to do with its spontaneity and the danger of doing it live," said Mitch one afternoon. "In a sense, it's an experiment to see what can be done with entertainment on television, what's *possible;* and at its best it challenges everything that television *is.* TV was getting so safe when *Saturday Night Live* came along; there was nothing out there, but *Love American Style* and *Gilligan's Island.*

DICK KLEIN

COURTESY OF FIREHALL THEATER

COURTESY OF THE GROUNDLINGS

A bove, John Belushi in Second City Days; far left Dan Aykroyd in Toronto's Second City; left sisters Laraine & Tracy Newman in The Groundlings; opposite, Bill Murray (Arab) in Chicago's Second City; coming up: cowgirl Gilda Radner.

"There's something incredibly ballsy about getting up, live, before twenty or thirty million people every week and doing complex comedy. I remember watching the first show and being amazed at how sophisticated it was. I wasn't always laughing—for the first few programs I was just trying to get a handle on it—but there was no way I was going to turn it off. For the first time in television comedy, it seemed to me that almost *anything* was possible."

The show's slice-of-life quality, fired by a zest for realism, gives *Saturday Night Live* its cutting edge of truth. The humor is daring and incisive, whether it be writer Dan Aykroyd and filmmaker Jim Signorelli's parody of a Navy recruiting commercial, in which the lowly swabbies are shown cleaning toilets; or Anne Beatts and Rosie Shuster's sketch about "Gidget's Disease," wherein grown women are stricken with terminal cuteness; or Tom Schiller's "Bad Playhouse" segments, in which stuffy theater critic Leonard Pinth-Garnell hosts an evening of poorly written drama. Unlike the overwhelming majority of comedy programs on the air, *SNL* doesn't cheat on the accuracy of its language, shrink from touchy, tough or sophisticated topics, or settle for what Michael O'Donoghue calls the "safe, bland, Dole fruit cup of most sit-coms." As a result, the program has waged a running war with the

DICK KLEIN

censors. And throughout, the work of each contributor retains a distinctive personal flavor.

What continues to be so appealing about *Saturday Night Live* as it enters its fifth wildly successful season is the intimacy of the show's comedy sketches, many of which are drawn from the lives of the players and the writing staff. This approach is the result of producer Lorne Michaels' determination to "find and create the show on the air," and also derives from the cast's extensive experience with and/ or affinity for improvisational theater.

From the beginning, the quality of *SNL* has been greatly enhanced by the work of Al Franken and Tom Davis, two prolific writers who also share a periodic performance segment ("The Franken and Davis Show") on the program. Franken is especially pleased with a 1978 sketch he and Tom did, in which Al's parents were invited on the air to share the limelight with their son. Unfortunately, Al was on a (simulated) ego/power trip that night and he ended up berating and then physically assaulting his mom and dad.

"Everybody yells at their parents," says Franken in retrospect, "so getting to do it on national TV was like a dream come true."

Franken and Davis, a veteran comedy team from Minnesota, were performing on stage in Los Angeles in 1975 with the San Francisco-based Pitchell Players when Lorne Michaels first spotted them. The Bay Area is the birthplace of The Committee, *the* seminal influence on improvisational comedy theater in America. No one in the *SNL* cast ever worked with The Committee but the impact of its acting techniques, in which humor was garnered from personal experiences and spur-of-the-moment roleplaying, is acknowledged by all members of the *SNL* company.

Other than Garrett Morris and Chevy Chase, all the Not Ready for Prime Time Players had improvisational training. John Belushi, Gilda

Radner, Dan Aykroyd, Bill Murray (and Bill's brother, *SNL* writer Brian Doyle-Murray), apprenticed with the famous Second City improvisational theater in Chicago. Laraine Newman trained with a Los Angeles group called The Groundlings, and Jane Curtin worked with a Boston outfit, The Proposition.

Behind both the Committee and Second City was the guiding force of a man named Del Close. "One of the things I do in my life," Close tells the actors in his improv workshops, "is turn my life into anecdotes." And for the self-confidence, self-awareness and comedic perspectives he has given to his students, they remain most grateful.

A CHILD OF NINE IS PERCHED

before the address pole in front of her suburban home as if it were a microphone. Dressed in a cowgirl outfit held up with a wide Western belt, she seems a pintsized Judy Canova, basking in the acclaim of a vast phantom audience.

Bowing graciously from the center of her lawn, the girl grins hugely and begins singing. Loudly. At 7 A.M.

"I asked my mother for fif-ty cents, to see the el-e-phant jump the fence. . . !"

She hasn't been out there five minutes when the phone inside her white-shuttered brick house in northwest Detroit begins to ring. It's the neighbors. Complaining.

"Hello! It's the crack of dawn! Does that kid have to do this *every damned morning?!*"

Twenty-four years later, Gilda still answers with a shrug. "I dunno why. I used to sing real hard too, but I'm not an exhibitionist; I was never doing it for anybody except me. When people were around, I'd go into the backyard and have a show there.

"With all the comedy work I've done for *Second City* and *Saturday Night Live*, it's so personal I still can't get used to people reacting to it. I'm surprised when someone comes up to me on the streets and reminds me of anything I did on the show. It's like someone catching me in my backyard when I was a kid playing. I'm actually embarrassed that they saw me."

Seated across from me in the back booth of a Greenwich Village beanery, is Gilda Susan Radner, 33, bright, undernourished and buttoncute. Her brown eyes dart from me to the top of a menu and back as she speaks with a squeaky insistence that is both adolescent and ancient.

Fiddling with the straps of her pink overalls, Gilda decides, over a succession of gin-and-tonics that she owes a great debt to improvisational theater.

"I think that anyone who is truly interested in comedy, and who is intelligent, knows about improv and Second City. I knew of it from the time I was finishing high school. I was thinking about it today, actually. When I was in the University of Michigan I was a theater major. I have held book for *Troilus and Cressida,* sewed the hem on a costume for the *Cherry Orchard* and been in the chorus of Greek plays, standing there and swaying—till I wanted ta *die* from it, ya know?

"But on the stage, see, me and this bunch of guys started this improvisational group called the Eastbound Mound, and we would perform in a coffeehouse in Ann Arbor. I think that when you have a need to be funny—and I *admit* to that—then you have to generate it yourself. There somehow isn't enough to satisfy that compulsive need, so you find people who want to improvise and you get together.

"I remember Second City came to Ann Arbor and they performed in the Trueblood Auditorium and I bought a ticket and sat in the second row on the right side. Someone sitting next to me said, 'You know, you should do that, Gilda.' It was true; I had Nichols and May's record albums, and I've always been a talker, and my only aspiration in show business was to be in Second City."

After catching a few more shows in Chicago, Gilda got the chance to audition: "You had to do five characters. You went up behind this curtain with somebody else, and you had to come out and ask whoever you were paired with for some information, resolve it, and then leave and come right back out as a different character.

"Well I *did* that," she says wrinkling her face in embarrassment, "and I kept coming back out in different characters, but real *hack* characters: an old lady, a teenager, a little kid. And then I had to sit there while the other person came out. This guy I was auditioning with, every time he came out he was the same guy, his characters had no definition. So one time he walked out, and I said, 'What, *you* again?!' And I got the job. That was a terrible thing to do, you know? But everybody in the audience was laughing."

"Anytime I do those personal, observations-from-my-childhood sketches on *Saturday Night,* like putting a crinoline slip on my head in the 'Judy Miller' sketches and pretending I'm a bride, you wouldn't believe how many letters of recognition I get! People say, 'I did that! I did that!'

"See, it's comedy without the mask," Gilda exclaims. "It's based on honesty and ordinariness. I'm not hiding behind a funny nose and glasses or a big production. I'm saying, 'This is *me* and this is what's vulnerable about me.' Those things are universal vulnerabilities.

"Our producer, Lorne Michaels, definitely plays off what's happening in everyone's lives, 'cause that is what's funny. If we don't have an opening for a show, he'll say, 'Okay, well Belushi's just come back from the West Coast and we're all worried he's gonna be a big movie star and turn into a jerk. Let's do a scene on that.'

"For the 1976 show Jody Foster hosted," she recounts, "I was not in it at all. I ran to Lorne and I said, 'Let me do the cold opening!' He said, 'Why? How's that gonna be funny?' I said, 'I'm not in the show. I want to tell my mother she can go to sleep. Why should she have to stay up 'til one o'clock and wait when I'm not gonna be on?' So Lorne let me do it.

"Somewhere in life, you find a way to cope with your own life by being funny about it," Gilda rules. "I've made the comic choice. And I allow people to *see* me doing that."

I'M BRIGHT AND I'M THIRTY-

five, I've been around," says a tanned, Chevy Chase, stretched out in his Hollywood home, several years after leaving *Saturday Night Live.* "I think my humor is subtle. But most of all, I believe it is *honest.*"

"I mean, I can't really lie without somewhere giving it away," he says sheepishly. "There's a little too much inbred guilt in me. A little too much Protestant ethic, a little too much Jewish guilt. Even though I'm neither Protestant nor Jewish but, as you know, a Muslim."

What the celebrated former member of *Saturday Night Live*'s Not Ready for Prime Time Players is saying is that he's the eternal wiseacre. Professionally, as he learned to play to the camera, "going through the lens and right into the viewers lap," Chase carried with him the same smartass sensibilities he had back in prep school.

"I remember we used to have a study hall with some 150 desks, and it was usually filled around mid-to-late afternoon. In the back of the room would be a professor making sure everything was completely quiet. I would enter and make as much noise as I could getting to my seat, knocking the books off other desks, banging into things, and then I'd do a spectacular fall."

As WRITERS FOR THE SHOW,

we're fortunate to be working with actors, many of whom are good writers, and all are good improv people," says Alan Zweibel, 29. "They're not afraid to embellish and expand the scripts, doing what feels comfortable for them, and personalizing their characters from the first read-through to the actual live performance. It definitely gives the show some special moments it could never otherwise have."

On Mondays the writers meet with Lorne and present their ideas for sketches, then work around the clock on Tuesdays getting the material ready for the Wednesday read-through with the actors. Zweibel explains the dynamics of the writer-actor relationship this way: "We do the initial casting, deciding who would be best for our material. The casting can change after the readthrough, depending on the actors' work loads in the various sketches."

Though the creation of a *SNL* program is a

The unfortunate Mr. Bill, a film creation of SLN writer, Walter Williams.

HANDTINTED PHOTOGRAPHS BY EDIE BASKIN

Laraine as Christie Christina, Garrett's Idi Amin, Gilda as Emily Litella and John's Samurai.

Bill as Nick, the lounge host, Dan's Tom Snyder, Jane as the Update anchorperson and Chevy as the Land Shark from Jaws.

Opposite: Nerds Lisa Loopner, Todd DiLamuca & Mrs. Loopner (Gilda, Bill & Jane); This page: Coneheads Connie, Beldar, Merkon & Prymaat (Laraine, Dan, Garrett & Jane), with Elliott Gould; wild & crazy guys Jorge & Yortuk Festrunk, (Dan with Steve Martin); Killer Bees, with Gould.

SNL First Families. This page: Dan as Jimmy Carter with daughter Amy (Laraine), Dan as "The New Dick Nixon" with Bill and Gilda as David and Julie Eisenhower; Opposite: John as Kissinger, Dan as Nixon, kneeling in prayer.

Ron Nessen with Chevy as Gerald Ford; Betty Ford (Jane) does a "Dance to the Nation."

cooperative effort, most of the writers go off to do the actual writing alone. However, some of the most popular characters were developed when writers worked in tandem with individual cast members.

"The Samurai character was one that John had when he auditioned for the show," says Zweibel, "and Tom Schiller wrote the very first sketch on the show, 'Samurai Hotel.' A few shows later Lorne asked me to write a 'Samurai Delicatessen' sketch. I was still moonlighting in a deli at the time, so I drew the details from my own job. Since then, it's just evolved with John and I working together on it."

Like the actors, the writers draw heavily on their own lives for comic themes. For example, Judy Miller, Gilda's gamine little girl persona, was created with Marilyn Miller, who not coincidentally has a younger sister named Judy.

Zweibel once worked with Sargent on a sketch for Chevy and Gilda called "After Love." Zweibel remembers: "The scene took place in bed after a guy and girl, who had obviously picked each other up at a party, had just finished making love. Thy're snuggled under the covers and Chevy says, 'Who's Phil? You mentioned him while we were making love.' Gilda says, 'Oh, I'm sorry. He was my old boyfriend.' Then she asks, 'Who's Terry? You said Terry in the middle of things.' Chevy looks at her and says, *I'm* Terry. Don't you remember? I told you at the party my name was Terry.'

"Well," says Zweibel with a laugh, "that kind of thing had once happened to me. I was in bed with this girl I met at a party—and she must've shouted out thirty or forty names before she got to mine!"

The backgrounds of the show's writers are extremely diverse. James Downey came to *SNL* fresh from *The Harvard Lampoon;* Marilyn Suzanne Miller had written for *The Mary Tyler Moore Show, The Odd Couple* and *Rhoda;* Tom Schiller was a documentary filmmaker; Anne Beatts was an editor of *National Lampoon;* Alan Zweibel had supplied material for a horde of stand-up comics; Rosie Shuster wrote for the Canadian Broadcasting Company and Lily Tomlin; Emmy Award-winner Herb Sargent had a long list of writing and producing credits which included *That Was The Week That Was.* Dan Aykroyd, Gilda Radner, John Belushi, Neil Levy, Al Franken, Tom Davis, Brian Doyle-Murray, Don Novello, Michael O'Donoghue, Brian McConnachie, Lorne Michaels, Bruce McCall, Chevy Chase, and Walter Williams complete one of the most impressive lists of talent ever assembled for a television show.

When ROLLING STONE Senior Editor Barbara Downey and I conceived the idea for this book, we knew it had to combine our collective enthusiasms for *Saturday Night Live* with a precise description of what makes the program so damned special. I myself could never quite put my finger on it. But one evening, while talking with Gilda Radner, she leaned over and said, "You know, I don't really think of *Saturday Night* as show business. When my father would take me to shows as a little girl, and I would look up and see the chorus line or something—*that* was entertainment to me.

"*Saturday Night* is something different, something that's more than entertainment, something that even feels funny to be paid for. 'Cause you know what it is?"

What?

"*It's secrets.*"

The first minutes of the first show, with John Belushi & Michael O'Donoghue: "I would like . . . to feed your fingertips . . . to the wolverines!"

EDIE BASKIN

THE
First Season

*BY
TOM
BURKE*

No one had been prepared for it: the first minutes of the first show offered no title, no credits, no music, only what looked like a professor's study containing Michael O'Donoghue, bearing himself as a language instructor. Enter John Belushi. Michael says, "Good evening." John shouts, *en accent,* "Good EVENING." That's repeated back and forth several times. Consulting his watch, Michael says, "Let us begin, repeat after me: I would like." John:*"I would like."* Michael:"To feed your fingertips." John: *"To feed your fingertips."* Michael: "To the wolverines." *"To the wolverines!"* Michael: "Next, I am afraid we are out of badgers." Each phrase repeated: "Would you accept a wolverine in its place?" Next, "Hey, Ned exclaimed, let's boil the wolverines. . . ."

Spent by this exertion, they both fall dead, and the show's begun. If you saw this and tried, the next day, to convey it to non-smoking nonwatchers, you cut yourself short with, "Well you *had* to see it." Most of *Saturday Night Live* can't be conveyed properly after the live fact. Though the audacity of its concept and execution, when played full out, alter not so much the visual and audio centers as the central nervous system itself.

WHEN YOU WAIT FOR *SATUR-day Night*'s instigator, 31-year-old Lorne Michaels, the first time outside his offices high in Radio City and he hurries past in the jeans and old cord jacket he usually wears, carrying a sandwich in a white bag, he could be from NBC's mailroom, or delivering from the deli. In no way does he appear charismatic, even when you enter his large 17th floor executive suite, not actually a suite but emphatically executive, a big corner office (in TV it's significant who gets corners), with views of both St. Patrick's Cathedral and Saks Fifth Avenue. On his executive desk are a pop art spilled-glass-of-milk and an antique toy NBC-TV remote-broadcast truck. Next to the video cassette

outfit, one bulletin board holds a complex map of the week's show in sequence, (they are going into their eighteenth show), another contains letters from famous admirers, like the one on stationery imprinted STEVE & EYDIE. The latter was written after an early show's satirical "Salute to the Coast Guard," which listed a number of people whom dolphins are smarter than. *Yes,* Steve and Eydie agree, dolphins *are* smarter than us! They do not exactly request here to guest host, though now a host of names would swim the Atlantic to be allowed to.

There's time to ponder this because Lorne's on the phone with the White House. Though *Saturday Night* (here forever more *SN*) doggedly makes sport of the president, Ron Nessen wants very much to be guest host this week. But it *is* Wednesday and he's still unsure whether the president can spare him. Lorne's demeanor toward Nessen exactly matches his demeanor toward everyone, as though he has determined that, because of his position, his pleasantness will *not* become graded according to anyone's status.

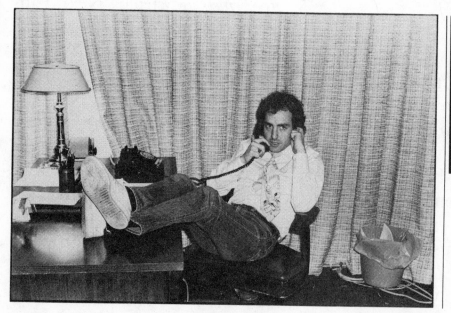

*L*orne Michaels in his studio office, left; opposite top, 5:30 dinner break in the Green Room; bottom, a president's view of marijuana with Chevy Chase as Jerry Ford rolling a square joint.

EDIE BASKIN

EDIE BASKIN

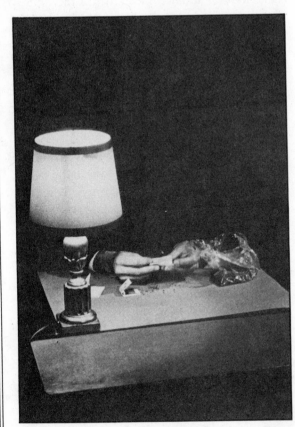

EDIE BASKIN

"Nice guy, Nessen," he offers. This is read, as is so much around *SN,* inscrutably. "Hmmm? No, I'm not panicked whether he'll come or not. I mean, I am. The show's written around him. This time of the week, we're *always* in a state of controlled panic. He'll come." In that, there's a sense of willed results which is startling.

Mention of Nessen reminds one to ask why, during a recent show's running gag titled "A President's View of Marijuana"–in which you see only Chevy Chase's hands on a presidential desk rolling first a square joint, then a triangular one, finally mashing a rolling machine in frustration–why an introductory "Hail to the Chief" wasn't used?

"No, no, that would have killed the gag's subtlety." Oh. One's suggested "Hail to the Chief" because of the persistent complaint that if eyes were diverted from the TV screen the instant the "President's View" logo was flashed, the point of the joke would be lost, you'd see only a klutzy joint roller. Stoically, Michaels shrugs, reflecting what will seem, in days following, a prevailing *SN* attitude, that subtlety's all, that here a gag is never milked, as it is in conventional TV, that if viewers are in the least square, dense or inattentive, fuck 'em.

"The *first* time Chevy did Ford," Lorne is saying, "it was because I love cold openings, no predictable introduction, except that we didn't have one and it was Friday night. As usual, we were pacing his office, desperate. Chevy suddenly said, 'Let me do Ford in the opening.'" (The way Lorne describes it implies that the renowned Chevy Chase fall was born, for *SN,* at that moment, but it actually evolved by mistake two years earlier, when Chevy was first writing for network TV, for the Smothers Brothers. "Tommy Smothers used to come into the writers' room," Chevy later explains, *"very* worried. He'd ask, 'What's *wrong* here?' I'd say, 'You're not doing anything that surprises anybody,'" and with a sleight of hand, so offhand you've missed it, Chevy knocks over the glass of Courvoisier beside him on his desk. "'See, that surprised you,' I told Tommy. 'You're not *startling* anybody anymore, do "The Fall of The Week!"'' The Smothers would say 'What??' So I'd say to them, 'Can I have a word with you?' and then fall over their entire desk. The unexpected.")

"So a great deal of what Chevy does now, solo," Lorne's saying, "I see for the first time during *Saturday Night*'s dress." *SN* does two shows every Saturday, the first a full-dress and camera rehearsal before a live audience about nine o'clock, and a second, live, aired performance at 11:30. "Sometimes I don't know at all what Chevy will do till we're on the air. He and [writers] Herb Sargent and Alan Zweibel, who work closely with him on 'Weekend Update,' are changing copy right up to air time. Chevy's very improvisational, sometimes he submits a whole script to me that's just one page with the words: 'me being funny.' Fine, the show is *built* on this, faith and chance, which are verboten in traditional TV." The latter's a phrase he'll use

repeatedly with vast, amiable condescension.

Encouraged to, he begins at page one of his life, and leisurely, for a couple of hours, he recounts it. But it can be summed up as follows: born in Toronto, he went to good schools there, writing, producing, directing and acting in school shows since before puberty. The summer after he graduated from the University of Toronto, he lived in a London flat with John Head, Howard Shore and Rosie Shuster Michaels, who are now, respectively, *SN*'s talent scout, music director and writer/wife of Lorne Michaels. CBC radio and television in Toronto employed him endlessly as writer/actor/director/producer but he got restive, moved south to perform his material at New York's Improvisation Club, which later nurtured Freddie Prinze, Richard Pryor and Bette Midler. "I had these very young messianic feelings about comedy then, I thought it should be of *use.* I've since learned it's basically for cheering you up." Jack Rollins, manager/Svengali to Woody Allen, caught Lorne at the Improv and hired him as a writer. "My first monologue for Woody was like a lot of stuff which crosses my desk now, about, I think, an eye doctor who only treats Cyclopes. We, my partner Hart Pomerantz and I, would sit in a room with Woody, the best comedy writer in the world, and talk ideas, and I thought, wow, *this* is what show business will *always* be like."

But ten years passed before it was like that again. "Woody didn't really need me, he was *teaching* me." Joan Rivers asked Lorne and Hart for monologues, eventually paying Lorne about $150. He acquired an agent at William Morris: "Dave Geffen, who was just then getting into music, he got us work writing an NBC series called *The Beautiful Phyllis Diller Show.* Our fare's paid to Hollywood, I'm given an NBC office there, wrote like crazy, every day network people came in. I'd ask, 'How's the show look?' They'd say, 'Great, *great!*' One day I drive onto the NBC lot, my parking spot's gone, the nameplate's been removed, in my office there are workmen *measuring*. 'Two guys can fit in here,' they are saying." The series, of course, had been canceled, but "the night they finished the first show, they actually had a champagne party. I still thought I'd really written something. Another writer said, at this party, quietly, 'don't you *know* it's shit?' This was a profound lesson, my first—how easily, in television, you can be seduced."

Candice Bergen appears, smiling, at Lorne's office door, then vanishes. "People who've done the show," Lorne explains, "Candy, Lily [Tomlin], they keep coming back, dropping in, it's fun here, etcetera. *Anyway:* while in L.A. I also wrote *Laugh-In,* not much, one season."

His war against traditional television really began then, in a motel in Toluca Lake. "That's where the *Laugh-In* writers wrote. *Separately.* You were doing this *taped* show, working six to eight weeks in advance, the process was, *is,* that of any big TV variety show: you handed in what you'd done to a head writer who then rewrote it to fit the star's style. Look, that's a very *valid* form of TV production." He mimes an extensive yawn. "But it was of zero interest to me."

About this time, he asserts venomously, it was announced to *Laugh-In*'s staff that Richard Nixon would appear on the show to do his now infamous "Sock It to *Me?*" "Paul Keyes, one of Nixon's speech-writers, was then *Laugh-In*'s head writer!" Lorne was ready to leave anyway: another kind of TV had occurred to him, a comedy-variety show in which the writing would bend to neither a star's schtick nor any preconceived format, a free-for-all in which various writers would always express *themselves:* "I envisioned this show in which all these individual styles were gotten across as purely as possible, with me clearing away the network and technological barricades. This is why *Saturday Night* must stay a *live* show, I've fought for that, to keep it *theater,* a pure communication between writers, players and audience. . . ."

Here, Chevy Chase, in an old shirt and sneakers, enters the office to mime the unzipping of his fly, peeing on the executive desk, and exiting with dispatch. Smiling indulgently, Lorne simply continues. "I went back to Canada." He and Rosie bought a house in Toronto where, he asserts, he had planned to live forever, working for the CBC. But L.A. remembered him, and he was offered the writing of a Burns and Schreiber summer TV show. It brought him west again, to other offers, and to live on the Strip, in the Chateau Marmont, where repainting never quite obliterates the lingering odor of grass. One afternoon he met Lily Tomlin. Their meeting lasted seven hours. "We'd been fighting the same battle alone: when technical people said, 'You can't do that because we can't shoot it right," she'd ask, '*Why?*' She was obsessed, dedicated, to infusing TV with something resembling wit."

For her special in November 1973, Lorne concentrated on writing closely for Lily. Though a network executive called the show "a $360,000 jerk-off," it won an Emmy which was, for Tomlin, another giant step and, for Michaels, his crucial first. He could not yet automatically command a table at Elaine's, but Tomlin was asking him to coproduce her next special, Shirley MacLaine was calling about her nightclub revue, and Flip Wilson was on the phone about his next project. Just as Lorne is now: Nessen's calling back.

The *SN* players, wondering, though not visibly concerned, whether or not their host's showing up, wander in—Gilda Radner, who does, among myriad characters, Emily Litella, "Weekend Update"'s querulous critic who questions all the media attention given to the preservation of "our natural racehorses, other horses need attention," and "Soviet jewelry, it's no better than ours," and "presidential erections, not a fit subject for the little ones." She's followed by Laraine Newman, who can imper-

RAIN WORTHINGTON

sonate anybody, notably Beauty Author Luciana Avedon, of the Camay commercials. Seated in a sleek, contemporary coffin, she smilingly asserts, "I was a hideous teenager, with fur on my ears and webbed fingers. Now I am young and beautiful. How? It is here in my *Beauty Regimen* book. How I drink the blood of Girl Scouts and Brownies. How I eat the faces of young virgins. It even tells how I have all my bones replaced with those of cheerleaders and pom-pom girls. Buy my book or I steal your lungs. . . ."

Lorne's office door is rarely closed, no one attempts to speak quietly here or is noticeably deferential toward him. They come and go freely: Garrett Morris, the black player who's shown sticking pins in a Chevy Chase doll. Danny Aykroyd, who's only 23 but does the brilliant Nixon impersonation. Actually, he and John Belushi write a lot of the material together, besides acting, but the network contracts department wants only so many people billed as writers. Besides Lorne and Chevy, nine are—Michael O'Donoghue, Anne Beatts, Tom Davis, Al Franken, Rosie Shuster, Tom Schiller, Alan Zweibel, Marilyn Miller and Herb Sargent. Lorne worked with or knew all of them before hiring them; several contributed to things like the *National Lampoon* (O'Donoghue and Beatts were editors), Marilyn Miller contributed to Mary Tyler Moore's show, *Rhoda* and Lily Tomlin, and Herb Sargent, the most seasoned and taciturn of them all, wrote Anne Bancroft's Emmy-winning special. More than 500 actors were auditioned for the rep company, but the only one

EDIE BASKIN

EDIE BASKIN

chosen who Lorne hadn't already known or worked with was Jane Curtin, the one who does the "straight" satirical readings, such as her narration, with Chevy, during "Update," of the Claudine Longet Ski Tournament, in which, just before all the skiers fall, rifle shots crack over the snow. ("Oh, Chevy, Claudine's gun went off again, by mistake, no, I think that time she'd been cleaning the gun and fired it accidentally. And that time, Chevy, Claudine had been showing her gun to a friend and . . .")

Not everyone's come into Lorne's office, but those gathered emphatically enjoy one another's presence; there's copious laughter, kidding, shouting, prodding, cuffing, embracing. When the noise obliterates his telephone, Lorne tolerantly motions them out, to gather in the larger rehearsal room across the hall for the group interview we've planned.

It seemed a good idea, this show being the ensemble effort it is; now, though, you almost, but don't, encourage them to postpone this session if they need the time to rehearse. It's struck you by now that at this point in the week, something, anything, ought to be happening to prepare for Saturday, with or without Ron Nessen. Why doesn't anybody seem at least dubious, or even slightly pressed for time? Certainly Lorne doesn't: though it's late afternoon, he determinedly concludes his own story before joining the others. While he's still languishing in Lotusland, Herb Schlosser, NBC's president and chief operating officer, hires Dick Ebersol, who's even younger than Lorne Michaels, to supervise late-night programming, and what Ebersol envisions, late at night, is a comedy show by and for the young.

This isn't as innovative as it sounds: NBC knows from its endless surveys that a huge audience, the 25- to 40-year-olds, don't watch prime time but do tend to stay home weekends, especially if they have good dope contacts. Offer them a head show, one to get high before, during and on, as high as its actors clearly are. Neither NBC, Lorne nor Dick Ebersol puts it just that way, of course; Lorne simply asserts that nowhere in videoland had he ever encountered an executive "with *my* same reference points, *my* humor, *my* resistance to TV formulas, *my* obsession with ... spontaneity."

It remained, however, for Lorne to do his real virtuoso turn, to convince board rooms full of NBC VIPs, who still bought Brooks clothes and ingested nothing more controversial than Valium, vodka and Kaopectate. "I expected to hear from them what they'd always said, about nobody understanding me in Iowa. But they didn't say *anything*. The wilder my ideas got, there were still no 'nos.' The final meetings were in, my God, New York, the anxiety capital of the universe. Still all I was getting were *nods*. I was getting a promise of 17 shows and they hadn't even seen a pilot! I was saying, 'We will always be experimenting, *on the air,* responding to our own mistakes.' I said, 'Show ten, *not* show one, will be the show to watch.' Schlosser actually replied, 'I'll watch show ten.'"

He's got to call Washington once more before our mass meeting, he announces courteously. Courteously, one leaves, to wander NBC's halls, to think. One has already observed rehearsal, dress and live performance of Tony Perkins's guest week, and the excitement of being close to these undeniably special people who create *SN* has palled just enough to assume—not quite correctly—that you've perceived pretty fully their troubles. Which are pretty much what you've been hearing from astute, impartial *SN* watchers. "Sure, they're funny, but not consistently enough. ... Their mistakes aren't already as cute as they seem to think ... Too much of the time they're just jacking off. ... Are too many people telling them they're clever? Three shows every 30 days, can't they edit themselves better, time themselves better in advance?" Lorne himself, has remarked that of all their shows, he really approved of maybe four. Though he won't specify which, Tony Perkins' is apparently not among them. Why shouldn't it have been? Perkins, professional, flexible, obviously delighted to be part of something so off the wall, has worked with a polished satirical style that ought to have perfectly matched *SN*'s. However (a) the opening monologue *SN* wrote for him was long and unpointed, (b) though the Norman Bates Motel School bit was fine, it was followed by an endless, strained sketch about the bad *Psycho* imitations moviemakers have forced him to do, and (c) he was forced into elaborate exchanges with the Muppets, whose leaden gaucheries rend *SN*'s comic fabric so cruelly one does wish them hacked to death with a kitchen knife.

Neither do the problems end there. As usual, two valuable time slots are given to a guest vocalist, such as Betty Carter on Perkins' show. As a jazz/blues interpreter she's seen better days, but even that's not the point; if the object is variety, why not always hire a singer with a satiric sense, like Loudon Wainwright or John Prine? And certainly Perkins himself could have been more thoughtfully, more extensively used. Chevy Chase is deservedly the star the show has made him, hilarious reading even the straightest lines straight-faced. But should his "Weekend Update" have taken *quite* so long, and should one of Perkins's sketches, about a sheriff's office operating the local teen hop, which read beautifully in rehearsal, be hacked, at the last minute, almost to death because the program ran eight minutes long in dress rehearsal? So the abominable "traditional" TV's taped; would *SN* so drastically compromise its integrity by taping just the difficult sketches and then editing flaws? In the Central and Western time zones, the show *is* seen taped—if live, it would have to run in prime time—and Lorne, et al., are very proud of the fact that a strictly unedited tape of what's happened live that night in New York is shown. So would it finally be so despicable to take out the turkey feathers? God forbid, of course, that *SN* should ever function with the factory precision of, say, *Carol Burnett,* but is the notion of *SN*'s writers starting to write at 10 a.m. Mondays, as Burnett's do, really so prostitutional?

When queried about this, Lorne's explanations are curiously incomplete. Audiences, he asserts, *like* the Muppets, no matter who else around here doesn't. Audiences *like* the comedy broken by music, and you can't always get the Loudon Wainwrights, because of their schedules, and because the budget around here isn't the Pentagon's. The show costs much more to do in New York than in L.A., there aren't the big sound stages here, the sets have to be built in Brooklyn and transported. And guest stars, whose regular fees *SN* can't pay, aren't usually available before rehearsals start, and the writers don't get sufficient time to know them or perceive the full range of what they may do best within *SN*'s context. "And the writers don't get in early Mondays because they know

they're going to work into the night all week. Sure, I ask for the material done by Tuesday, but there's always some formal excuse why it isn't. If people have gone off Sundays, to, uh, live their lives, whatever, and have gone without sleep and schlep in here Mondays wrecked, you can't expect of them instant brilliance." He doesn't say it, but you feel here he's felt it pedestrian of me to suggest that the Muses may be coerced into scheduled materialization. "Tape? *No way!* Live laughter from an audience is real, it's theater. With tape you've got to fake it, postsync it, it sounds dead, canned, like laugh tracks." For the first time detectably defensive, he concludes, "Look, what's occurring here *already* is a fucking technological miracle—that we have not slipped back into being 'television.' If anything's fucked us up in recent weeks, it's been the press. It was Eden here for close to six months, there were *no* ego free-for-alls, then certain performers started getting all this press mention. Sure, it's caused tension. Maybe this group interview we're going to have will air some of that. . . ."

Not bloody likely, it turns out. In the big rehearsal room, where nearly everyone's gathered, you quickly sense a resistance to the meeting; lately they've been trying hard, Lorne's explained, not to take themselves too seriously. Nobody in this room wants to sound to anybody else too glib, for the press. Also, you sense they've all got plenty to say that's not to be said in front of Lorne Michaels.

Silence. "Jesus, what a bunch of dildos," somebody offers good-naturedly. Gilda Radner cooperatively begins, "There is *this,* that nobody can *stop* you, like, they can *never* say, 'Cut, start over.' " She talks through a laugh, as if on speed, but it's only her high good humor. "It's *pure* theater, but for this audience of *22 million!* Incredible! Like, we've all done theater, but for *22 million?* You can't *think* about 'em. It's exactly like being onstage, you concentrate on character, you don't count the house, the camera eyes can*not* speak 22 million to you, but somewhere in your head you know they're there, you're reaching so many with your work. *Right as you do it!* For an actor, there's nothing like that, *incredible!"*

But Laraine Newman has spread herself on the floor, her lips caressing the tape recorder's mike. In her nasal newsperson voice she says, "Actually, Gilda's right, Tom, the little eye does not, *nawt,* speak 22 million to you. . . ."

"Actually, Tom, the show is taped, the live thing's all a big lie." A writer has cut in with that.

"Wrong! It's the most fun you can have with your pants on."

"Actually, Tom, it sucks, and we all, in reality, hate each other."

Danny Aykroyd sings, in a light-opera parody, "Tom, we came here, from all over this great land, Garrett's from Lou-i-siana, Gilda, she's from De-troit, there's a couple 'a Canucks in this big video bar-rel!"

Chevy hasn't laughed during any of the above, he's looked mostly abstracted. Watching him the past week, it's crossed your mind that he's not a happy man, or at least that he's too easily taken lightly. Tony Perkins, listening to Chevy play the piano during a rehearsal break, has remarked, "God, he even does *that* well. He's the kind of personality they're always watching for in this business. Incredibly attractive." True. Then what, other than the malevolence directed toward any seemingly brash new star, has conditioned you to suppose him shallow, except that (a) you've not really talked to him alone, and (b) his continual satirization of himself, of his own ego, has not at first been easily comprehended. Also, you've heard too many *SN* watchers complain that he's "funny, yeah, but he looks so self-infatuated." Being around him, however, you've sensed that he could be, besides the smartest of *SN*'s staff, its most thoughtful, most complex member.

What he interrupts with, gently, is: "Tom, you can't expect to conduct some kind of group encounter here. What's really wrong

EDIE BASKIN

EDIE BASKIN

This page, Dan Aykroyd's Howard Hughes wears the aerodynamic bra he designed for Jane Russell, played by Raquel Welch; opposite, Tony Perkins with the Muppets.

EDIE BASKIN

here, nobody's about to say it in this room. There's a lot of stuff. We all *know,* for example, that too many things which play stunningly in dress rehearsal often bomb in the live show. As the Green Giant says, there's this moment of perfection at which things must be picked, and we don't hit that moment often enough, too often we're playing something very well in dress, *knowing* it will *never* be this good again. For one thing we're getting too confident. When you get the great laugh in dress, you're too secure in it, throw it away, then, live, it bombs."

Lorne cuts in rapidly. "Chevy, that's often just a simple matter of timing, we can correct that." And he changes the subject to the matter of the "'soft' pieces, which are stylish and quirky but don't get assured laughs, sometimes because we haven't chosen the right week to do

them. There's a lot here we write and do hold until it seems topical—like 'Dance to the Nation,' where Betty Ford's doing a dance-advice show. That piece only works if she's *done* something that week. As opposed to a 'hard' piece, the *sure* laugh, like John as the 'Update' weatherman. . . ."

AT THE CONCLUSION OF "weekend update," Chevy courteously introduces "our chief meteorologist, John Belushi," for the seasonal weather report. In a vaguely Tom Snyder-esque wig, John begins, "Well, another winter's almost over, and March, true to form, has come in like a lion and, hopefully, will go out like a lamb. At least, that's how March works here. But in Norway, for example, March comes in like a polar bear and goes out like a walrus. Or take the case of Honduras, where March comes *in* like a lamb and goes out like a salt-marsh harvest mouse. Let us compare this to the Maldive Islands, where March comes in like a wildebeest and goes out like an ant. . . ."

He's getting very febrile here, on the edge of mental collapse. Chevy tries to interrupt, to no avail. ". . . How unlike the Malay peninsula, where March comes in like a worm-eating fernbird, and goes *out* like a worm-eating fernbird—in fact, their whole *year*'s like a worm-eating fernbird! There's a country where March hops in like a kangaroo, stays a kangaroo for a while, then it becomes a slightly *smaller* kangaroo, then for a couple of days it's sort of a cross between a frilled lizard and a common house cat, then it changes *back* into the smaller kangaroo and then it goes out like a wild dingo! And it's *not* Australia! You'd think it would be Australia, but it's not!"

Chevy continues to try to stop him, but he's totally out of hand now. After mentioning the nine different countries where March comes in like a frog and goes out like a golden retriever, John has a heart attack and succumbs under the "Weekend Update" newsdesk.

THE MASS MEETING HAS DISIN-tegrated by the time "Dance to the Nation"'s merits and shortcomings are considered, and Chevy and most of the others have quietly exited. It's clear now the *SN* people ought to be talked to, or eavesdropped upon, separately, or in small groups, but that doesn't happen immediately. For one thing, Ron Nessen does show up, and one remains very peripheral to his show. "We're *not* endorsing *any* candidate, of course," Lorne's stated, but the Nessen week, though funny enough, appears to be either *SN*'s blatant Washington ass-kiss, reciprocation for everyone being asked there for dinner the week before, or a thorough duping by the

White House of *SN,* which produces on Saturday a long slow-motion replay of Nixon's Sock-It-to-Me. Ford himself has lots of spots (taped) on the show; never has a president so benevolently blessed, in front of millions, those who make sport of him. It's disquieting to watch, and you expect the next week, starring Raquel Welch, a funny, camp, professional performer, to be an oasis.

It is and it isn't; in a way, it's a repeat of Tony Perkins week. Welch, closely scrutinized, seems the soul of happy cooperation. Like Perkins, like Dick Cavett, who dissents only with Lorne's obsession with live work vs. taped ("For a long time there I *did* do taped shows which looked and sounded live, it's not *that* impossible to pull off, I don't think audiences really think about, know or *feel* the difference"), like Buck Henry, who speaks of *SN* as does a young father of his first son, Raquel Welch is genuinely exhilarated, riding this maverick, and when you talk to her in her hotel after the show, she's clearly pleased with it. And she's decidedly no dummy. "It was all my idea to be on there, I saw just a swatch of it one night flipping channels. Next day I called my manager and said I'd seen this mad thing and didn't know what it was, but if they were looking for a guest, I'd love to. Lorne came to see me, I told him that more than anything, I'd like to come out in blue jeans and not be this idiot screen goddess, you know? Just hang loose and get down a little. I told him that, unfortunately, I didn't have any prepared stuff, like Lily Tomlin or Richard Pryor, but I could see he had great writers, and I hoped they'd want to have fun with this joke *I've* had to live with, the sex-symbol number. Which *is* funny to me. I did tell Lorne, 'Tit jokes are fine, but if we do *too* many, I know from experience they'll just sound mocking to, you know, Middle America, and women in general. They'll get too childish, end up boring.' "

No, they didn't do too many, "Truthfully, I

liked what happened around there, the final result was good. I had no intention of trying to take over the show as a star. I'd seen that the whole point of me being on there was to work with the company, express myself in a way people haven't seen me, but to keep the presence always subtle, you know?" Pause, frown. "I do think the next time I do it, and I'd like a next time, that Lorne and the others will know me a little better, be more confident that I can do comedy, which I'm not sure he was. . . ."

Canny Raquel: though Lorne doesn't say so, he wasn't, and neither were the rest of *SN*. You've talked to them separately; their cavils they don't much want quoted, individually, but some of them do seem markedly restive. Nobody can stomach the Muppets, really, or the dull guest singers. "Lorne's still too locked in to a variety format, no matter what he says," somebody grumbles. The consensus is that the players, when they're working together as comic actors, not celebrity-guest pawns, could hold the whole show by themselves. This is probably true; they are, en ensemble, that good. But guest names, as Jane Curtin concedes, *are* important, for things like ratings and to draw the hinterland viewers and just for breathers, between laughs.

Gilda Radner's more expansive. Of the women players, she's had the best public response; privately, she's the most articulate, and bewildered. *"Sure* there are tensions around here," she starts. We're in a room close to Lorne's but she doesn't lower her voice. "There are ego problems every day, just like a family has problems, y'know? The Emmys are swell, but they aren't going to ease tensions. You know what *does?* Like when I'm upset here, I *cry,* we *all* cry in front of each other. When I'm mad at Laraine I yell at her, when Chevy's on my nerves or I feel jealous of him, I *tell* him. We *all* do this around here, it gets rid of the evil. Also, we all make each *other* laugh all the time, which is what makes the audience laugh,

which is why the show's a success. The format's not new, and Sid Caesar was live—it's the quality of the minds here, but with the creative flow comes an *ocean* of neurotic energy. I said to somebody the other day, everybody who works here's a baby, and like children, we're all still going through kid changes. Michael O'Donoghue, he has a good sketch idea, he runs out of his office jumping, clapping his hands in the air, like a kid who's just discovered a turtle in the backyard! Then we all go in to Lorne and dance it out for him, like showing your dad your new party dress, like you go in to your mommy and say, 'Hey, I found this stone outside that's a diamond.' "

Though she can talk nonstop, Gilda's also a listener, a real one, and you find yourself telling her that to grasp the full focus of *SN* has been remarkably tough. Nodding, she says, "Tom, it's because, for one thing, while we're all kids here, nobody's a sheep, there's no one performer who couldn't carry a *whole* show by himself, no one of our writers that couldn't do a major project alone. There's so much individual strength here, it's driving *everybody* slightly nuts. We're *all* saying. 'Wait a minute, I'm a team player but I'm not, I'm an individual!' There's weeks when *I* feel like the star here, the next week it's suddenly like I'm in the chorus line. For all of us, that's a real difficulty to live with. This show's not an ideal situation for an actor. Partly it's just the nature of TV. You get so creatively frustrated! You do a scene once, it's gone forever, you have no way to perfect your art. Or, like, I love doing Emily Litella, I'd love doing her *every* week, but they tell me, 'Let it rest awhile, they'll get sick of it,' and I swear, a part of me dies, even though they are *right*. And if we're good actors, and aren't realizing our potential as actors on this show, then, yeah, something *is* wrong. . . ."

How about the fact that, except for Chevy, she's gotten more audience response than anybody on *SN?* Even Gilda's frown is attractive.

"Yeah, but ... look, first, the job itself has a way of keeping you incredibly repressed. Since I'm only using a fraction of the ability I have, since I'm just giving here, a little taste of it, the attention I do get I don't feel I deserve. Not for *this* work. If I'm getting known, I have an incredible problem about it anyway, I thought about this. Know what it goes back to? School. No kidding. I'm from Detroit, went to the University of Michigan, there was this sort of big diagonal outside on the campus where all the kids sat around. And I was petrified to walk through the diag. I'd go four blocks out of the way to avoid that. I was afraid I'd be noticed. And talked about, that somebody'd say, 'Look at *her* outfit.' *And:* I was *just* as much afraid I *wouldn't* be noticed! Okay, so now, I go out on the street, some days lots of heads turn, it's 'Hey, Gilda, hi, Gilda, I *love* you on the show!' Some days I love it: it's why I *wanted* to walk through the diag! Other days I want the four blocks to walk out of the way. ..."

Her grin's a lamp snapped on in a dark room. "Confused, right? A kid neurosis: I know I can make people laugh; at the same time, I have no special technique, I don't study a character. Doing Barbara Walters, on the show, I didn't do hours of research on her, I just tried to pick up on what I thought was the one thing that's funny about her, her vocal

EDIE BASKIN

EDIE BASKIN

*O*pposite: some early writers, left to right, Lorne, Tom Davis, Alan Zweibel, Michael O'Donoghue, Al Franken, Anne Beatts, Tom Schiller, Rosie Shuster, Marilyn Miller, Chevy Chase; this page, Candice Bergen as Catherine Deneuve & Ron Nessen in makeup for guest host appearance.

thing." And she does it, straight-face. " 'This is Baba Wawa, today ouw special guest is a famwous speech thewapist who'll teach me how to pronounce the name Harwy Weasoneh.' It was my idea to do the bit. And I don't have to *think* about those bits. I often feel guilty, 'cause I know actors really have to study, they're supposed to take it *seriously.* . . ."

Decidedly, John Belushi does. Of all the players, he's the most vocally seditious. Around the show, the idea of pretending to fire the Muppets, or taking pretend gunshots at them, has been discussed, but just for comedy. John, more than anyone, would like them fired in reality, and relishes the notion of shooting them with real bullets. Also, Lorne and Rosie Shuster created the concept of the players dressed, in many sketches, for no discernible reason, as bees. Mention that, and John pounds his desk with a fat fist. "What we *are,* man, is actors. And this show's good when we're working together, all of us, in a sketch, as comic *actors,* playing off each other, *with* each other, *not* reading cue cards, like we have to, but

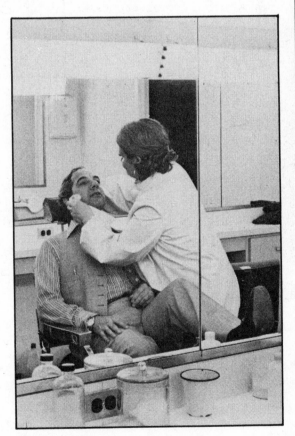

EDIE BASKIN

memorizing the lines in advance, making eye contact, not dressing like fucking *bees!* You can*not* put an actor in a bee costume and say, well, that funny dress will make up for the weak writing. Sure, they'll laugh at the antennae once or twice, after that, forget it, it's repetitive shit, *I hate the fucking bees!*"

We're alone in the little office he shares with Danny Aykroyd. Even when he shouts, which he often does, the sounds of Illinois gently alter his vowels. Born in Chicago, Belushi grew up in Wheaton. "No, nobody in my family was in show business or anything, they were just, you know ... people." Like a number of the *SN* people, he doesn't seem to want to talk much about home, the past, and you don't press him. "I guess I always wanted to act, I did, like, from junior high on. Why? Well, I was into sports, high school football and all, because it was a way of getting two things I wanted: attention and girls. And acting was another means to the same end."

Maniacal grin. The night he went into the city from Wheaton to see the Second City troupe firmed up his plans. "Great, man, they were funny *and* smart, I didn't know actors were both. And they were *acting,* it knocked me out." He got somebody to ask if Second City would let him audition, they said no. "Who the fuck is *he?* was the reaction." But he stayed on, hanging out in Chicago, and eventually backstage at Second City. "Sometimes at one or two a.m. they'd let me walk on in an improvised bit, finally a lead guy left and I started doing main parts." He stayed two years, then was called upon to write and act in *National Lampoon*'s *Lemmings,* at the Village Gate, New York. His incomparable Joe Cocker imitation, which stopped the show, was really what started him on *SN.* Bring up his current employment and his face progresses through a series of remarkable, somber mutations.

"Look, I think that now, we, the players, have become, well, bigger than some of the stars who're booked as hosts. Like, after we won the Emmys, the first show happened to be Buck Henry's second host spot. When he was *first* on, people said, 'Who's he?' TV audiences didn't know from him. But *after* we won the Emmys, that show with Buck was the highest rated show of the year. So were they there to watch him, or us?"

Of course *SN* now has, more or less, a star in-residence, doesn't it? The smile is not a grin. "Well, NBC loves Chevy. Plus, he's very good. Look, *I* love Chevy, ever since *Lemmings,* we were in that together all through it, we work great together, Chevy's a good *actor.* I think he's better in sketches than in all those bits as this Chevy Chase persona; in acted comedy as opposed to presentational crap. But Chevy holding the show as star, I don't think it'd work. It sure wouldn't be the same show. I know I want in *no* way to become Carl Reiner to his Sid Caesar. Once we bend to a fucking star system here, everything changes."

Paradoxically, change in *SN* is what continually rings in John's monologues, like a well-wound Westbend. "Some of the continuing bits now, we're just jerking off over and over. What I see now is taking the whole show as it is, throwing it out, and coming back with a whole new concept! Get rid of *all* the old standard characters, the stale stuff, catch phrases!" He doesn't specify but he means Gilda's Emily Litella, Jane Curtin's slick interviewer, even "Weekend Update." "Lorne's pressured, because, sure, the network, like always, wants to go with a winner as is, but fuck 'em, we've got to build on what we've learned this year, see how far we can *reach.* Like when I did Captain Kirk in the *Star Trek* takeoff, I had to turn this dumpy little body into William Shatner, commander of the Starship Enterprise, and I spent, sure, a couple of hours in makeup, but man, I *did* it!" and he does it, moving in the small room, doing Shatner's cool walk magically. "Makeup doesn't do it, man, you gotta *act* it. Maybe here we can become total *actors*. But you can't, if the next fucking moment you got to get into a fucking bee costume. I want to *burn* those fucking bee costumes! We're not little windup animals. If that went on and on here, *sure* I'd leave. The fucking guest number—listen, every one of the players sings great, Gilda, Garrett Morris, Danny, everybody, so instead of bringing in, like Esther Phillips, why can't one of the *group* sing? If there has to be this host, I'd like to see each one of *us* doing it, in rotation, one week's host is Chevy, next week Gilda, next Laraine, right? The Emmys give us the leverage to carry that. . . ."

But while *SN* is still saddled, for nonartistic reasons, with guest-star hosts, shouldn't they be considered more profoundly? John and others of the staff rightfully resent the Richard Pryor show, as Pryor insisted on bringing along his own writers and entourage, to lard the evening with his now tiresome ethnicity, and Paul Simon more or less turned his night into a Paul Simon concert. But Candice Bergen, who's hosted *SN* twice, was genuinely funny, especially as Catherine Deneuve, the Chanel bottle attached to her head. ("It ees not easy being Catherine Deneuve. You theenk it ees a funny joke to be a beeg, beeg movie star who is so beautiful like me, Catherine Deneuve? I must get up early in ze morning even eef I was to ze party wis Omar Sharif. I must be photograph for *Vogue* magazine. I must fly all ovair ze world and stay in ze luxury hotels, and sometimes zey do not even have ze mineral water. I *hate* being Catherine Deneuve!") It's startling, and sad, when one of the players says, "My God, movie stars, what does Candice Bergen put on her passport? Actress? Except she can't do that much. Writer? But she doesn't do that very well. *Comedian? That* could get her in trouble with the State Department."

A similar attitude prevails regarding Raquel Welch, who's been fine in, for example, an Anita Bryant orange-juice commercial parody. "What's a Florida sunshine girl like me doing in Beirut?" she asks, being tied to a post to be shot by a firing squad. "Spreading the good word about orange juice! Sure, there's a war, strife and bloodshed in the Mideast. Internal chaos can be *such* a hassle. But even this war-torn country enjoys Florida sunshine!" Her reading of *"such* a hassle" is funny enough to carry the sketch by itself, but the bit doesn't make it onto the air. As usual, Saturday's dress rehearsal doesn't end until ten. Instantly, Lorne, who supervises every moment of the show behind the cameras, closets himself with Dave Wilson, a slightly older, seasoned professional who's billed as *SN*'s director but is actually its technical expert, in charge of finding, with Lorne, the smoothest ways to quickly cut the 10 to 20 minutes the show's run overtime in dress. By 11 or so, Lorne's gathered the cast and writers in the Green Room to fire off an incredible number of complex cuts and changes they'll be doing live in half an hour. ("Chevy, speed the opening, it's running 2 minutes, 30 seconds, rush the fall. Garrett, Gilda, they can't get a mike boom to you on the first sketch, you've gotta shout the lines. Danny, your music cue's cut, Raquel's first speech is cut, Danny, your speech on page 15's cut, Gilda, cheat more to the door, John, the following affects the future of civilization as we know it, with Raquel you've got *no* single shot, *only* a two-shot, which *won't* happen unless you're *exactly* beside her there." Etcetera.)

The actual show, however, is rewritten until it's unwieldy, and doesn't get the laughs it should. This is also true of the sketch in which Raquel plays Jane Russell to Danny Aykroyd's Howard Hughes—he's designed an aerodynamic bra for her—and the one in which Raquel's a sexy Nurse Ratshid in a *Cuckoo's Nest* movie sendup called "One Flew over the Hornet's Nest," with the rest of the cast dressed as bees. Backstage, you've noted, before

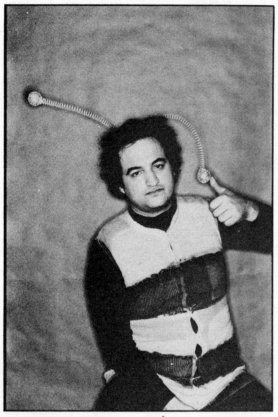

EDIE BASKIN

the week's even begun, a certain negative resignation. Though everyone's careful Raquel shouldn't feel it, the attitude is "What're-y'gonna-do, we've-got-this-*movie-star*."

Something Lorne said, abruptly, uncued, during the group encounter, has stuck in one's head. "This show was conceived as a *starting* place for people. Like off-Broadway, from which, inevitably, people want to move uptown. Writers here will get tired of writing for a live audience. Performers will want things where more ... discipline's involved. Sure, those people will move on. I have to decide whether to keep the show changing for the needs of those who've originally created it, or just let those people leave to do other things. The show is *only* valuable as long as the people here get off on it, get out what they have to say. As soon as anybody starts staying because of loyalty, or some similar fucked reason ..."

Pause. All eyes are on him. Sadly he adds, "I think we've been through our grace period, doing just a show *we'd* all enjoy watching. But when you're trained in that *other* TV system,

RAIN WORTHINGTON

This page, above, bee John Belushi; left, Star Trek sketch with Dan as Scotty, John as Capt. Kirk and Chevy as Mr. Spock; opposite, Chevy Chase in T-shirt statement.

this is ... Jesus, such exhilaration, the simple fact that we *exist*."

What this has been is a sort of plea for no one present to out-grow him quite yet. Still, it's happening, and he knows it. It's struck you that after weeks of research, *SN* still remains somewhat a conundrum, and that the answers to its questions, perhaps ultimately unanswerable, might lie with Chevy Chase.

"You could come over to my house to talk," he offers. To quote Chevy accurately is to make him sound obsequious, which he never is. You have watched for this. What he is is friendly and accessible by nature. He's aware that his presence is personable and disarming, has probably always known that, and always distrusted it. At least he does not visibly use the knowledge to his advantage, except, perhaps, before an audience. "You could come over here, except it's just a mattress, really. I live here, you literally have to live this show, it has to become home," and he blesses the room with his glass of Courvoisier. The walls of his office, placed strategically closest to Lorne Michaels' though a sixth Lorne's size, are hung with an awful picture of Tom Snyder, satirically signed, in Chevy's own hand, "Keep up the good work," and one of Chevy shaking hands with President Ford–except the photo's been embellished (by *SN*'s artists, at Chevy's request) with strange Middle Earth graphics and the faked signature, "Sincerely, Gerald Fuck/Fart/Ford." And he's framed his astrological chart, which shows, besides his birthdate, October 8th, 1943, various planets diametrically opposed.

"So how you doin'?" He asks this because one has sat silently a few moments. He knows that his grin, too, is compelling, and maybe untrustworthy. As with Lorne, you start by asking him to be autobiographical, which doesn't much stimulate him. "I was married very young, when I was 24. Divorced, there's nothing more to say about that. Except that I've been with a girl who lives in L.A. for quite

a while now. Sure, we've talked about marriage. Talked. Tom, I hope you won't print this. Her name's Betty Ford. No, her name is," and he spells it painstakingly, "Jacqueline Carlin."

Playing with pencils, he states that his father's an executive at Putnam's, the book publisher; that his parents separated when he was young and both remarried and had more kids; that he grew up mostly with his mother in New York, "upper middleclass, WASPish, a sort of hectic, wired growing, fast and slow at the same time. I *always wrote*. Went to a lot of schools, do you really care? Okay, P.S.6, Dalton, Haverford College, Bard, various graduate stints, pre-med, education, English, meanwhile playing in several rock groups, keyboard and percussion. Somewhere in there, I actually

EDIE BASKIN

got a degree in audio engineering. Truth. I sang, wrote, directed, produced and acted in *Groove Tube,* the film, and did all the same things for *Lemmings,* the *Lampoon* off-Broadway show. I was *thinking* about acting then. I really wasn't when I wrote for Alan King, just after *Lemmings,* or when I wrote for the Smothers." Here he pulls from a file cabinet beside his desk a foot-thick pile of pages. "That's what I wrote for the Smothers that did *not* get done. I proliferated that, it was cathartic. I thought writing was all I would ever do."

But people kept seeing him under the kliegs. "In L.A., these agents kept trying to sell me to TV as, I dunno, Baretta or something, there were a billion of me out there. Yeah, it did shoot down the ego somewhat, I guess I did want it." When Lorne asked him to do *SN,* though, it was strictly as a writer, and he didn't instantly accept. "I'd already learned how to deal, I kept upping my price, and upping it, to, yeah, a figure higher than the other writers'. Still I didn't take it, because I *had* said to Lorne, 'I want the option to perform some of what I write.' And he'd replied, 'No way, you're an unknown acting quantity to me, I'm hiring a rep company to act, you write.' So I took it on that basis, but I was with Lorne while he auditioned all the actors, helping him decide. He made everybody do a sort of screen test for the show, and asked me to do one too. Which led to his asking me to do 'Update.'"

His face twists sardonically, acknowledging the you-asked-for-it aspect of his current dilemma. "Listen, I am sure as hell not asking for sympathy here. I know fucking well I won't get any, either. There are these people who'd kill to be where I am now. What would I tell you, getting an Emmy, even as a supporter, means nothing? Balls. I liked it a lot. I *don't* think it'll make a difference beyond where I am, I mean, it's leverage, in the business, but I do not think an Emmy will spoil Chevy Chase. Any further. I did *not* know what to say,

accepting it, that's the truth. The acknowledgment, the acclaim, I sure as hell never *discouraged* it, this 'star' number that's happened. But what I still am is a *writer,* and because of this other thing, the writing's getting *fucked,* I'm not turning out anything like what I did at first, I'm suddenly this *commodity.*"

Here he waves a letter from a lawyer who's proposed suing somebody who's making Chevy Chase T-shirts without authorization. "As Lorne said to me this morning, 'You're now putting in six to seven hours a day being Chevy Chase whether you like it or not.'" Everybody's aware the network does like it immensely, and would be quite at a loss if Chevy suddenly decided not to appear on *SN.* Its wishes aside, he's not really entertaining that notion. "Shit, you're drawn to this *attention,* you wouldn't be human otherwise, but Christ, I don't even *like* actors. From the start it's been so fucking important to me to communicate, *as a writer,* my vision of life. As an actor you're just doing somebody else's, I also hate the fact that acting's the most tenuous, gratuitous profession imaginable. I hate how self indulgent actors become, that they lose all perspective, you're unable to see yourself anymore except as what agents and the press tell you you are, you no longer feel. And, the worst, that you lose the ability *to listen.* Jesus, listening, you know this, it's *central* to writing, and you're no longer doing it, it's all me-me-me and you've stopped listening to your wife, lover, children. Christ, this is a nightmare Orwell never dreamed of. Not listening equals not understanding equals not feeling, and when that happens, fuck it, you might as well hit the grave."

A secretary's entered diffidently with NBC publicity photos for him to autograph and he is clearly embarrassed that this should happen while I'm present. He tries to laugh. "Tom, I swear, I did not plan any of it. Being a television star, and–*Jesus!* I can't believe I just used those words, that asshole cliché! When I have spent the last ten years as a writer *commenting* on that cliché, shitting on it, satirizing it. So how long can you poke fun at it after you've *become* it?"

Because he is, again, genuinely troubled, as opposed to dramatically, you wish to ease him; however, you remark here that, having observed hundreds of actors it seems probable that the cliché called stardom is, for better or worse, something which occurs as if destined, that asking for it or not ultimately has little to do with it happening. He listens to that carefully, and considers again.

"You think that? Yeah, I know what you're trying to say. Something is happening like that to me, resist it, it happens anyway. I can feel that, the vibes are there. What am I going to do about it? I *don't* know. First, we've got part of the summer off, I've now *got* to get away from here, see if I can get enough perspective back. What's humor, written humor, any humor, but a sense of perspective, priorities, values? Jesus, meeting Ford, you saw the ultimate cliché there, you're looking 50 milligrams of Valium in the eyes, he's totally sublimated by tradition, he *cannot* do what I've *got* to do, step back, see if I've got any perspective *left*."

And if he hasn't? He's silent for a while, studying the wall to his right which separates him from Lorne Michaels. "Look, my contract here ends this September 15th. From the beginning, I wanted it that way, no way would I be locked in on paper for five years, like a lot of the people here are. And in September, yeah, I could be gone. I'd go, for one thing, if this show doesn't keep changing. I *cannot* continue being typed here as just this funny newsman character, or a fall guy. I still love the fall—it's started feeling stale to me, burnt out, like my

writing here, but it's still tempting, you know? At the same time, the only thing interesting about comedy is surprise. So I leave whenever this show becomes *Laugh-In.* Or *Saturday Night.* As soon as it becomes safe. I don't mean safe in the sense that we don't get the hell started earlier in the week, early Monday, or do the show *alternate* weeks, maybe then we'd have time to do it right. I have been *fighting* for that."

He glances to his right again. "I know what I would *like* to happen: that I'm smart and sane enough to use what's happened here to me correctly. For leverage. To get . . . power. Shit, I don't like that word much either. Hitler was first to understand that word in a media sense, all those huge loudspeakers, when he addressed the masses, like the musicians at Woodstock. What I mean by power is that of a man who's writer, performer, director and producer, and if I can get, through what I have now, all those things at once, then maybe what I had to say back there when I started all this could get translated into a valid, valuable finished product. That is my point, assuming I'm making one."

Sure, by now, he's had offers from elsewhere, lots of them. And his objective can't happen here, there's already present one commander-in-chief. "Listen, when you write about all this, don't be hard on Lorne. He is, underneath, truly a teddy bear you wanta hug." Chevy is smiling. "Oh, Christ, what the fuck am I doing here, being interviewed? Listen, everything I said to you just now is a lie."

He has meant this to be funny, and it is. The plaintive knocks on his door have become more frequent, and he must go, to be a commodity, within one, for now at least.

EDIE BASKIN

THE
Players

EDIE BASKIN

GILDA
Radner

*BY
ROY
BLOUNT JR.*

YOU KNOW THAT STOFF YOU find in your eye?" Bushy-haired, outgoing *(bushy-haired! outgoing! pale words!)* TV newsperson Roseanne Roseanadanna extricates from the corner of her eye some of that strange, crusty matter—that stuff that we all have known intimately, which our

mothers may have referred to as "sleepy dust," but which we have never really faced up to that dubious mystery of, and which we never expected to hear mentioned on *national television.* . . .

Roseanne looks at this stuff, makes a luminous face of distasteful fascination and exclaims: "You look at it and you say, 'What *is* this? This stoff came outta *me!?*' And you hold it between your fingers and you roll*lllll* it around, and roll*lllll* it around, and you think, 'What amma gonna *do* with this? Where amma gonna *put* it?' And you roll*lllll* it around and roll*lllll* it. . . . And then it don't matter

EDIE BASKIN

what you do with it. It's *gone."*

Before I made Gilda Radner's acquaintance, I doubted it would be too good an idea to roll around and roll around whatever stuff it is that comes out of her when she becomes Roseanne—and Emily Litella, Judy Miller, Rhonda Weiss, Lisa Loopner, Baba Wawa and all kinds of other awful but peculiarly fetching characters on *Saturday Night Live.* I was afraid Gilda would be less redoubtable than her characters, that she would be neurotic, mostly, and would let slip that she is so funny because she used to be fat and has never gotten over it (I got this impression from research); and then she would run and throw up; and there we would be—she explicated, I brought down.

But no. Fat is a factor, and Gilda is a waif, but her stuff will stand some rolling around.

SHE IS WALKING DOWN SIXTH

avenue in her strange tip-tip-tip ... tip-tip ... tip ... tip-tip-tip teeter-wobbling fool's progress manner, which is accentuated by high heels and tight Levi's. She has just left a place where some of her oldest friends in New York can be found: her dentist's office. Many a time she has sobbingly confided her nondental problems to Dr. Paul Scheier (who on request will do Swedish-dentist and Indian-dentist dialect) and his assistants. And once, after Dr. Scheier had temporarily removed her many caps, she ran outside on Central Park South wearing her drool bib, flashing her tooth stumps and holding two of those absorbent cotton cylinders in her mouth like fangs, banged on his ground-floor window and cried in a demented voice, "Give me my teeth! Give me my teeth!"

But before we go on, let me just summarize briefly what Gilda Radner looks like in person going down the avenue:

(a) all of her characters

(b) a fresh-faced, young, good-looking woman

(c) a regular, more-than-ordinarily sympathetic person you would have no reservations about going up to on the street and asking if you had some spinach caught in your teeth, or something, if you had to know

(d) a second grader who (1) has just been told she can have a puppy, and is pleased as pie (2) has just been told that her puppy won't live, and she can't understand why.

She squints a lot and has a scratchy voice and she chews: "I'm on gum. Sugarless, a whole pack. And if I can chew all this sugarless, I can throw in one stick of sugared. I have very bad teeth," she adds. "It's something about the saliva in my mouth. . . ."

EDIE BASKIN

"Hey Gilda!" "Hey Roseanne!" young persons along the avenue are shouting. She responds nicely, not as a star, but as a fellow young New York pedestrian who *happens to be* a star. And sometimes celebrity can be a nuisance.

"I've had people get mad at me when they see me on the street. Like, 'What are you doing out here?' They're going, like, 'Oh, a star,' but with resentment. Kids come screaming after me down the street, and I tend to forget—you know, I'm on my way home or just going for cigarettes, just doing my life? And they all want autographs and I say, 'Isn't it enough that you *saw* me?' I mean, I'm ambitious, I'm greedy for attention. . ., but, isn't it enough that they *saw* me?

"I'm a big starer. I went to read for that movie *Girl Friends,* and while I was waiting there was this girl who had on this Marimekko print dress that matched the color of her tights *exactly,* and she had the biggest tits I ever *saw,* and I stared at her so long I didn't get prepared to read and I gave this terrible. . . . I just murmured the lines.

"And now everybody stares at *me.* When you take away a comedian's opportunity to observe. . . .

"But I don't understand people who say they can't be funny in real life because it would use stuff up. That's like saying you can't write but so many songs because there's only so many notes. I can always make that choice—I mean, when somebody comes home and asks what went wrong today, I can either tell him the truth, you know, I'm depressed, I'm . . . Or I can say, 'Well, the maid had jury duty and couldn't come in today and her brother-in-law from North Carolina came instead. . . .' You know, and make up stuff. Making that choice. Because I have lots of energy.

"I saw Woody Allen at a party, and I couldn't *stand* it, because he was just standing there, not talking to anybody, and I don't know him but I love what he does so much, and I went up to him and *pushed him in the chest.*

"And it was awful. Because *he didn't like it.* He didn't say anything. ... And I said to people who knew him, *please,* tell him I was just. ... And he probably–the terrible thing, he probably didn't even notice. You know what I mean? I say 'You know what I mean?' a lot.

"But ... Sometimes ... One morning I changed clothes 800 times, I really did, I really wanted to look attractive. I really wanted to look sexy. And I went out and a guy went by in a truck and yelled, *'Hey. You're funny.'* "

She makes a pained face. "Hey Gilda, why do you walk funny?" asks this young guy who comes up behind us.

"I have a very uncertain walk," she says.

IRA RESNICK

"But that's all right. So does my brother; he's in real estate. Hey, you walk pretty funny yourself," she says to this guy.

"Yeah, I'm in the *Guinness Book of World Records* for it," he says. "I walked like this all the way from Hartford." And he disappears, walking that way, into the distance.

"Hey," she says. "That wasn't bad."

GILDA GREW UP IN A COMFORT-able suburb of Detroit, the well-loved daughter of a man who did so well in real estate and investments that she inherited serious wealth herself, I am told, when she turned twenty-one. Her father dreamed of being a song-and-dance man and took Gilda to Broadway shows, and he died, of a brain tumor, after years of just lying there, when she was fourteen. She has never gotten over it and doesn't like to talk about it. Her mother was a frustrated ballet dancer and a great beauty who gave Gilda the impression that she might have been expected to be more beautiful herself. For one thing, Gilda was a fat girl. She went to girls' schools and camps where she was the funny fat girl with a heart of gold.

At the University of Michigan in the late Sixties, she worked in theater and avoided politics. "My friends would try to get me into things and I'd say no, I have to do this play. In fact I moved to Canada when pepper gas came through the window."

She lived with a sculptor in Canada, trying to be a homemaker, but it didn't work out. Many boyfriends have come and gone, including actor Peter Firth and fellow *Saturday Night* star Bill Murray. "I don't know whether it's me ... sometimes, or it's them. ..." She doesn't like to talk about it. But she keeps saying she wants to be a wife and mother. "And pretty soon I'll be over thirty-five and I'll have to find a man who's willing to father my mongoloid children."

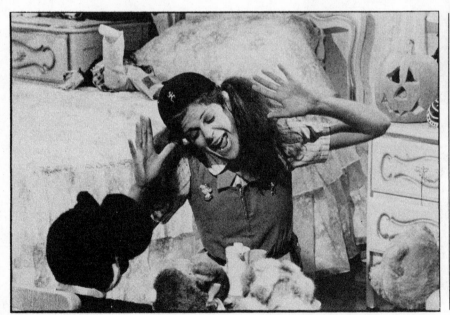

Opposite: Gilda as a celebrity, pictured here at an office party; this page, top, as Lucy with Desi Arnaz; left, starring in the "Judy Miller Show."

EDIE BASKIN

She got into comedy professionally with Toronto's Second City improvisational troupe, then the *National Lampoon Radio Hour* and in 1974, the *National Lampoon Show* onstage.

"In London, Ontario," says Bill Murray, "we were supposed to do the show twice a night to two different audiences. But there was only one audience's worth of people in the whole town. And they hated us. But one night, all of a sudden as we turned around, we heard this cackling. This girl in front was laughing! And we looked out and it was Gilda. She had sneaked away from us and down into the audience. And we realized that if *we* were watching us, we'd be funny. She gave us the will to go on against this nasty, ugly crowd.

"In New York we did the show to a really hostile crowd. Came to curse at the actors. Gilda was great. She did 'Rhoda Tyler Moore,' playing a blind girl trying to make it in New York. John Belushi was her boyfriend, and he'd change his voice and pretend to be these thugs hitting her. Beating her, cuffing her around on the stage. Then he'd change back to the boy-friend's voice and pretend to be saving her from the thugs. Then he'd pretend to be a big dog humping her, and then he'd chase the dog off. . . . It was really funny, and she'd die with this wonderful blind face, this wonderful smile. She'd run, with a cane, full speed into this wall. To get a laugh. She was covered with bruises. You had to admire her."

By this time she was thinner. Lorne Michaels was forming *Saturday Night Live,* and he hired her without an audition. "I had known Gilda in Toronto and thought she was real special," says Michaels. "She was the first person I picked for the cast. At first, she said, 'I don't do characters,' and I said, 'Well, I don't do windows.' Now I think she's right there between Charlie Chaplin and Lucy—and I don't mean to say she's got one foot in the grave."

"She's probably the best physical comedienne ever," says *Saturday Night* writer Marilyn Miller. "She can do literally anything. Doing the 'Judy Miller Show,' she fell off the bed and smashed her ribs up and kept going."

The "Judy Miller Show," scripts by Marilyn

This page, Gilda as nerd Lisa Loopner, going to the prom with her boyfriend, Todd DiLamuca, played by Bill Murray; opposite, Gilda as Tammy Widette.

EDIE BASKIN

EDIE BASKIN

Miller, is a running *Saturday Night* feature wherein Gilda, in a Brownie suit, is acting out in her bedroom a major one-person entertainment. No jokes, just this eerie re-creation of a five-year-old disporting herself, murmuring, "and then I go . . ." and "ta-da-ta-daaa," and sort of singing and sort of dancing, all alone.

"Gilda is very much in touch with her child self," says Miller.

"Yeah, sometimes almost too much," says Gilda. "When I'm doing Judy Miller, it's amazing how my mind clears away. I have to just completely forget about whether people are looking up my skirt, and just flop around and be five."

A skinny five. "Funny is the thin side of being fat," says Miller, who, like nearly all of *Saturday Night's* women writers and performers, used to be fat and constantly worries about being fat again. "If you've ever been heavy, there's always a fat person standing behind you saying, 'You're fat, you're fat.'

"I wrote a song for the show, 'Goodbye Saccharin,' when it looked like saccharin was going to be taken off the market. That was written by me in utter panic. And sung by Gilda, as Rhonda Weiss, in the same way. Linda Ronstadt heard we were going to do it and volunteered to sing backup because the subject was so close to her heart. Even Laraine Newman, who's eighty-three pounds, holds the tops of her thighs and says, 'Ewwww, *jodhpurs.*'

"As girls, we were all fat and loud. If you can talk real loud, maybe people won't notice you're fat. It's like one side of the world is thin and attractive and the other side is fat, loud and funny. We look toward a new world where everyone can be thin, attractive, fairly loud and rather amusing."

Gilda even seems to prefer her *material* thin. "The worse the material is, the better she does," says Murray. "She's really fearless with stuff. We sent her out there as Howdy Doody's wife, Debbie Doody. That was it: just being Mrs. Howdy Doody with some strings hanging off her. *Deadly.* And she was *great.*"

Gilda has gotten thinner and thinner—to the point now of fashion-model skinny—and more and more prominent. Since the departure of Chevy Chase, she and Belushi have become *Saturday Night's* best-known regulars (just recently, Gilda won an Emmy for best leading actress in a comedy variety show). It's to the point now that she is getting movie and TV-special offers and is recording her own comedy album. On her album cover, she says earnestly, she wants to look like Donna Summer.

SOMEBODY SENT ME A TOENAIL, okay? In the mail." She is sitting at her desk—

EDIE BASKIN

Left, "Beach Blanket Bimbo" sketch—Princess Leia (Carrie Fisher) meets Annette (Gilda) and crew; opposite, Debbie Doody, Howdy's wife.

she has a desk—at NBC. The toenail was a, response to the Roseanne routine in which she talked about toes—"you know how your baby toe looks like a canoe, and . . ."

On her desk is *Julie Eisenhower's Favorite Stories,* selected from *Jack and Jill* and other children's magazines. But what Gilda is looking at is *TV Guide,* which has just come out with her on the cover. "I'll be like a coaster in millions of homes of America. All week, people will be putting their beer on my face."

Another thing that has just come in is a new comic book in which Gilda and the rest of the *Saturday Night* cast are rescued from terrorists by Spiderman. "Hey, I don't even look Jewish as a cartoon. I look like kind of a neat girl with big tits!

"When I started out in the show, I told Lorne, 'Every character I do is going to be this Jewish girl from Detroit. I don't do dialects; they all come out like Swedish.' "

But one day she and her friend and co-star Jane Curtin "were fooling around," and Emily Litella came out. Emily was based on a woman named Dibby who took care of Gilda when she was a girl. Emily, supposedly responding to Jane Curtin's editorial, would go on at great length demanding to know why people were making such a fuss over, say, "Soviet jewelry," until someone would break in to tell her that it was "Soviet Jewry."

"Oh," she would, of course, say, "Never miynd." A great sound in that "miynd." The *wangy,* ratchety tones of Gilda's characters linger earphone-deep. Who of her fans cannot summon immediately in his mind's ear the last note of Roseanne's recurrent exclamation, "Ah thawt ah would *dah."*

But the Roseanadannaism Gilda thought would prove most catchy is what Roseanne says her father always used to say to her: "He used to say, 'You know, mah little Roseanne Roseanadanna, it's *alllll*-ways *som*thin.' " That is what Gilda's father always used to say to her.

Gilda's characters have a wonderful imperviousness. Especially Roseanne. Writer Rosie Shuster got Roseanne started in a "Hire the Incompetent" bit—Gilda was the blithe, overwhelming bewigged incompetent talking about making hamburgers, and you know how sometimes an armpit hair will get into the patty? . . .

After that, Roseanne became one of the "Weekly Update" newscasters, but somehow her reports always swung around to some new bodily grossness. Gilda and writer Alan Zweibel work out the Roseanne skits together, often over lunch, so that facial-sore references and phrases like "rectal eclipse" mingle in with their sandwiches.

I always assumed that Roseanne's name, at least, came from Roseann Scamardella, the unWASPy coanchorperson on New York's Channel 7 news, and rumor has it that Scamardella was recently given a raise to some 90 grand a year because she had become identifiable to the point of Roseanna-dannafication. (When I caught her on TV the other night she was saying, "Amid the rats, dead cats, garbage and feces. . . .")

But Gilda says the name grew out of "The Name Game," a favorite song of hers whose refrain goes "Bannana-banna-bofanna," and that she developed Roseanne as an antidote to "all these women reporting the news on TV; they always look like they're so frightened to lose their job. You know they're saying. 'We're women and we have credibility to report the news, we don't go number two, we don't fart'—they're like these perfect. . . . And Roseanne, she'a a *pig*. Under the table she's wearing the highest pair of heels and white socks, she's Jewish/Italian/Puerto Rican. . . ."

And she is nice. She has a magnetism. She accepts her body. Gilda's characters are people you enjoy knowing.

"Yes," says Gilda, "I'm always there. I'm thirty-two years old. I like people. I like my job. That person who loves doing it is always in there. And I don't want you to miss the joke. I'm in there taking care of you while I'm doing the job."

She says that Michael O'Donoghue—the *Saturday Night* writer and occasional performer whose quintessential bit was his portrayal, with the assistance of backup singer, of Tony Orlando and Dawn having their eyes put out with red-hot needles—"gets on me for being cute. He says it's all right now, and it'll be all right when I'm old, but when I'm middled-aged, it won't work."

Saturday Night Live might tip too far toward the mean and spacey, however, without Gilda's

EDIE BASKIN

niceness. Her "Baba Wawa" takeoff on Barbara Walters, though biting, is hardly nasty. Baba has such a presence, even if she does say "wee-wee" instead of "really."

Gilda put Baba's voice and mannerisms together not by studying Walters directly, but by asking other people, "What does she do?"—focusing on "the things that stand out about her for other people. One time I saw her at a party. I went up to her and said, 'I'm the girl who does you on TV.'

"And you know, she's very tiny—but very tough; she's on top of everything. She took me over into the corner and said, 'Okay, what do you do?' And I did some Baba Wawa and she watched, saying, 'uh-huh, uh-huh,' you know, and, 'Yeah, I'm working on my *ehw*'s and *ahw*'s.' "

Saturday Night Live is right down Gilda's alley, and its personnel are, to a great extent, her family. During the *Saturday Night* season, Gilda is around the studio all week and all hours, studying the camera blocking, helping writers work things out, making people rehearse with her, bringing them into her personal crises (once she put a notice on the bulletin board: "Lorne: I'm happy"). When she goes home, she sleeps with her phone in the bed so she's ready when a writer calls up in the middle of the night to tell her he's figured out a line.

But even though the show's ratings are great and it has won an Emmy, its people live in some anxiety that each year will be its last. The cast is mindful of the fate of so many old *Laugh-In* stars: occasional daytime-panel shots. "Whenever we do something really cheap in rehearsals," says Gilda, "Lorne starts whistling the *Laugh-In* theme."

Gilda is surely well enough established that she will go on to do her own shows. But if she is to aspire to the level of Lily Tomlin, Gilda will have to develop her independent repertoire further. She is working on that now for her

album, with a mind to taking the same material on the college circuit.

"But comedy albums—that's one of the saddest sections in the whole record store. They don't even have fingerprints on them. What I'd like would be for my album to be played in a supermarket—if they would play my album over the PA system and people would shop to it."

She could see getting into movies, but so far her only film role has been a bit part in *The Last Detail.* She appeared, plumply, in a scene where a group is chanting a mantra and meditating and talking things out. She was supposed to stand up and say something about a breakthrough she had made in playing the clarinet. But by the time the cameras started rolling she had come to like the Nichiren Shoshu group so much that she arose and gave a testimonial to the chanters' supportiveness.

"So finally the group chanted that I would remember my lines, and I did."

Her first love, she says, is the stage. Two summers ago she appeared at the Berkshire Festival in *Broadway,* a play starring William Atherton and Chris Sarandon. "I was enjoying their acting so much I was just leaning back being lazy, thrilled that I was getting to be an ingénue with them."

"She was camping it up," says a prominent critic who caught her performance.

Gilda says: "After he saw the show, Lorne told me, 'Don't you ever embarrass me like this again.'

"I guess it will come down to doing some kind of television. I grew up in front of a television, I guess I'll grow old inside of one."

"HOW OLD AM I?" SHE ASKS HER
makeup man.

"Oh . . ., early thirties," he says.

There is a silence.

"I look my age," she says.

FRANCESCO SCAVULLO

"No you don't, no you don't," cry the makeup men and the hairdresser and I.

We are in the dressing room of Francesco Scavullo's studio, where that famous glamour photographer is to shoot her for the cover of ROLLING STONE.

There are pictures all around the walls: *Cosmopolitan* girls, various eminently glamorous or decadent personalities, Arnold Schwarzenegger naked, a man with a skewer in one cheek and out the other. This man has his mouth open so that you can see the skewer passing through, and he appears to be smiling. There is a small, vaguely shaggy dog running around everywhere. "He's a King Charles spaniel," says a woman who works there. "He's Oliver Twist. Isn't that right, Oliver? You're twisted."

The makeup man and the hairdressing man are devoting over an hour and a half to preparing Gilda for her portrait. She had arrived nearly an hour late, with no makeup on and her hair just washed and floating, looking keyed up and saying, "I think I look ugly today." Now she is having her eyebrows plucked and her hair layered so that it sort of tendrils out exotically in various directions, and her face layered painstakingly but thickly with paint.

"What *is* this?" Roseanne might say about all the different tubes of junk in the makeup man's kit. "This stoff gonna go onto *me?*" But Gilda is avid for glamorization. The idea had been for her to pose as Roseanne, but she insisted on being shot as herself, as beautiful as possible.

The girl her mother wanted. Gilda says she and Laraine Newman have the same kind of mother—beautiful. Their mothers didn't want them to have blemishes. They went into comedy to protect themselves, she says.

"My mother was exactly the same," says the makeup man. "That's what messed me up." He catches a look of himself in the mirror and sighs, "By this time of day I look worse and worse."

"Did you want to be a movie star when you were a little bitty girl?" I ask.

There is a silence.

"Are you talking to me?" Gilda says.

The makeup man and the hair man, who are the only other parties present, smile.

This is the first time I have seen her without her green jacket with the teddy-bear pin on it. She really is skinny. "I saw myself on TV and couldn't stand it, I looked chubby," she says. "So I lost weight, and now people say, 'You look awful'—my arms and everything—but now I look normal on TV." She holds up her arm, which looks underfed, and flexes it, so that it looks anatomical. "I like it! I can see all my muscles and everything."

"Can one of the boys, uh. . . . ?" The hairdresser asks a woman who works there, indicating all the hair on the floor. "There aren't any boys," says the woman.

"Here, I can get that for you," says Gilda—only kidding, only kidding, but seemingly the most amenable person around. She wrinkles her brow, forming four horizontal lines. "Draw in those lines and draw on a clef," she suggests.

There's an idea! Let's use all this makeup to bring Gilda's real stuff out! Let's paint a pointedly exaggerated but still amicable smile on her mouth and that musical-worry design on her forehead and a well-earned bruise on her chin.

Or let's step back and let her move into some kind of makeup freak character, who cries; "More! More! I can still see my nose! I hate my nose! Cover up my nose! Do something with my tongue! Here, let me eat some of that! Pour it down my neckline! Eyes! More on the eyes! *I want more languorous eyes!*"

But Gilda says she hasn't "reached the point where I can tell people what to do yet," and anyway, she is not going to pass up a chance to look divine. Like a cute little car with a lot of chrome on the front, she enters an all-white room and lies on the floor, and Scavullo shoots and shoots.

WE GO TO DINNER. SHE EATS her own four courses and portions of my last two. I tell her people want to know how she lost weight. She hasn't been looking forward to this question. "Here it is: I had a cyst removed from an ovary and lost ten pounds and kept them off. So tell everyone: chew a lot of gum and have major surgery. And I do jumping jacks. And pretend I'm jumping rope. If you use a rope, you miss and it breaks the flow. I put on records and dance."

Roseanne might be more forthcoming. But Gilda is intent upon keeping some stuff private. "I want people to like me," she says, "But the more people who like you, you realize how you want just a few people to like you. Who you can phone. Having the world love you is not gratifying. Because you don't know their phone numbers.

"They all applaud, but none of them will come home with you and look at your back someplace to see if you have a pimple.

"Show business is an opportunity to pretend. And to get scared. And to not be mediocre. Get everybody to look at you. And you get to make people feel stuff, you know. I've got to work just as hard at that with one person as I would with 40 million people.

"I'd get real scared if it started being *only* for 40 million people." She looks real scared.

"I have a boyfriend now who's an actor, who I'm going to see tonight after his show. Wait . . . I'd better make a phone call to see if . . ." She begins to rise. "No," she sits back down, "it's all right. I do have a boyfriend."

Even Roseanne makes Gilda uneasy. "People want to peg you," she says. "I don't care if I ever do Roseanne again. I'd rather force myself to come up with someone new."

When I ask her about the disadvantages of being a woman in her line of work, she rolls earnestly into a *girl-power* statement: "When I was a little girl, I said, 'Gilda, are you glad you're a girl or do you wish you were a boy?' I said, 'Boys have to go in the army, get in mud, wear heavy stuff and kill people.'

"I love being a woman. You can cry. You get to wear pants now. You can *always* sit and think when you go to the bathroom. If you're on a boat and it's going to sink, you get to go on the rescue boat first. You get to wear cute clothes. It must be a great thing, or so many men wouldn't be wanting to do it now.

"One great thing about not being superior, you get to change yourself. Wear high-heel shoes, make yourself taller, put makeup on.

"And you get to give up.

"That's all."

However all this stuff may look in print, on hearing it I wanted to adopt her, order her another meal, buy her beautiful fuzzy bathroom slippers. What I did was blurt out, *"Gilda I thought you looked pretty when you came in, before they put all that makeup on."*

She makes an I-could-just-cry-except-it-would-seem-maudlin-in-the-story face.

"Bill Murray says you would run head-on into a wall, being a blind girl," I say.

"Yeah," she says. "I'd throw myself into it. *I don't want to die.* I have a real strong will not to bomb. I want to do the job well, not waste anybody's time on the job, not waste anybody's time who's watching. And not jerk off."

AFTER DINNER SHE LEAVES IN A cab, looking worked up, and I stand there on suddenly less-intense Second Avenue, reflecting that I would like to see her run at a wall sometime and that it would dissolve and she would go right through it and sail off to some better place where blemishes are jewels, weight is immaterial, *Saturday Night* is immortal and she is loved duly by the right number of people.

I reflect that, but I don't really mean it. I want to see her bounce.

EDIE BASKIN

BILL
Murray

*BY
DAVID
FELTON*

IT'S THE BOTTOM OF THE
ninth, the last show of the first
season for rookie Bill Murray on
Saturday Night Live, and it looks
like the new kid from Wilmette,
Illinois, may be in trouble. Frankly, ladies and gentlemen, Murray
has been going through a little
slump since he first joined the

Not Ready for Prime Time Players club in January 1977. A heavy
hitter from the improv leagues of
Second City and the *National
Lampoon*'s off-Broadway revue,
he's had trouble adjusting to the
peculiar disciplines and timings
of television. Now it's Wednesday morning, the day of the read-
through for Saturday's show, and
in a few hours all material must
be completed for final judgment.
And Murray, a writer-slash-actor,
doesn't have a thing in his head.
He steps in the shower, picks up
a corny, microphone-shaped bar
of soap that Judy Jacklin, John
Belushi's wife, gave him for
Christmas . . . and suddenly a gut

force consumes his being, a clutch instinct, something he may have learned from playing baseball as a kid, or playing basketball in high school, or dealing suitcases full of dope in the early Seventies. When the going gets tough, the tough get funny. "Hmmm," he thinks, examining the soap, "what if . . .?"

Murray suits up, races down to NBC in Rockefeller Center, grabs Gilda Radner, and together they write a script in twenty minutes. It calls for a running shower, a soap microphone, a naked Murray, a naked Radner and a fully clothed Buck Henry. The production people balk at the shower, say it can't be set up, but Bill fights and pleads and finally they relent. And that Saturday night the viewers see one of the wildest pieces Murray has done:

[*Bill enters shower and draws curtain. He is very up, but shivering.*]

BILL: All right, okay, another day, another dollar, Richard Herkiman, let's go. [*Claps hands*] Come on, let's go, let's go. Letsgo letsgo letsgo. Haaa! [*Turns on shower*] Hoga hoga, haaa, heyaheya, ho! Boy, that's cold. Cold! That Mexican family's gotta go! Oh! All the hot water's gone. Okay. [*Picks up soap mike and speaks into it, raising his voice*] Ladies and gentlemen . . . Richard Herkiman. Hey! Woo! Thank you, thank you very much. Woo! [*Starts to sing, nightclub style, snapping his fingers, rolling his eyes, wagging his lower lip, as water gushes over his hair and face*] "Well there's something in the way that girl moves, that attracts me like no other lover. Yeah, there's something in the way that she moo-oo-ooves me. . . ."

GILDA: [*Pokes head through curtain*] Honey. . . .

BILL: [*Part announcing, part crooning*] Ladies and gentlemen . . . "don't wanna leave her now" . . . a very special guest . . . "you know I buh-lieve, and how" . . . my wife, Mrs. Richard Herkiman, Jane Nash! Come on in, Jane. [*Leads her in*]

GILDA: Honey, will you quit fooling around. . . .

BILL: Dah . . . da, dah . . .

GILDA: I just want to take a quick shower, all right?

BILL: Say, Jane, how do you feel about singin' a song today, huh?

GILDA: Richard, will you quit fooling around, I'm just taking a *shower*.

BILL: Aw, come on, honey, would you mind singing that wonderful morning song? [*To camera*] Come on,

let's hear it for her! [*Studio audience actually applauds at this point.*]

GILDA: [*Reluctantly sings, her face dripping*] 'On a clear day, I will walk around you, and you'll see"—Oh Richard, stop it, you're being silly.

BILL: Listen, honey . . . a lot of folks out there wanna know . . . if you really love me—do you honey?

GILDA: [*Increasingly irritated*] Would you . . . leave me alone, Richard, come on!

BILL: Do you love me with your whole heart and soul? Come on, honey.

GILDA: Yes, I luvya, I luvya, I luvya.

BILL: I know this is corny and old-fashioned, but come on—there's nobody else, is there? You really love, honor and cherish me, don't ya?

GILDA: I love you, now leave me alone, I'm in a hurry.

BILL: [*To camera*] Well, you know, folks out there, what my wife doesn't know is that I know she's been cheating on me for the last couple of years and . . . we've got behind the curtain a surprise guest, the man she's been seeing behind my back for the last two years. Here he is—Richard Cularsky! Come on in, Richard, good to have you aboard!

[*Buck Henry enters in coat and tie, shakes hands and stands between them under the shower.*]

GILDA: What are *you* doing here?

BILL: Yes, I brought him all the way from his home in the city to be with us here today. Isn't that terrific?

BUCK: [*With game-show exuberance*] Something tells me I shouldn't have come. But I do love you, come what may.

BILL: Now tell me, kids, you kids must spend a lot of time in the shower together when I'm not here. Huh?

BUCK: You bet! Naw, it's funny—I'll tell you the truth, a lot of people have the wrong idea about that. It's actually a lot safer to rent a hotel room. You know, there's much less chance of meeting an aunt, or an uncle. And you don't have to worry about changing the *sheets* on the *bed*.

BILL: [*Laughing*] Ouch! I forgot how much is involved in this kind of thing. Woo! Well . . . honey, you've been confronted with this thing now. Are you gonna break it off with him for the good of your marriage, or are you just gonna continue to stick the knife in and twist it and twist it, huh? ha ha.

GILDA: Ah ha, yes, Richard that's exactly what we're gonna do, ha ha.

BILL: [*Laughing*] Wow, that hurts. Ah ha ha ha. *Okay*, you'll have to excuse me, but I'm an emotional guy and . . . I really hate to get bad news, I'm sorry but that's the way I'm built, *okay*. Gee, I'm afraid that's all

EDIE BASKIN

EDIE BASKIN

Previous page, Bill as Richard Herkiman interviews his wife (Gilda) & her lover (Buck Henry); left, unaired "What If" sketch, Bill as priest with Jane & Garrett; bottom, as entertainment critic on "Weekend Update"; opposite: as "The Honker," a wino, with Dan.

the time I've got for today–thanks, kids, for dropping by.

BUCK: Before you finish, Richard, I just want to say that we'll be in Philadelphia the first week in June at the Statler Hotel.

BILL: Ah ha, great. Well, I'll be looking for you there, okay? Thanks for stopping by–Mrs. Richard Herkiman and the guy she's been messin' around with. Woo! [*Audience applauds.*] Thank you everyone.

The ninth-inning shower scene was a huge success, the kind of tour-de-farce that has established Bill Murray as a comic actor of uncommon subtlety, depth, wit, dexterity and something crazy about the eyes. "It was like graduation," he recently recalled of his clutch performance. "It was one of those real hard entertainment things where you really have to go crazy, selling it hard, to make it work." As Jack Brickhouse, the Chicago Cubs announcer whom Murray loves to imitate, might put it: "Hey, when you come by, bring me my stomach."

EDIE BASKIN

THERE'S SOME DANGER IN-

volved . . . something in Bill's eyes," says Lorne Michaels, producer of *Saturday Night.* "When he does a character, he'll go all the way with it. He's very similar to Lily Tomlin—he wouldn't say so himself, probably—or Richard Pryor. All his characters have real integrity." Steve Martin, a frequent *Saturday Night* host, agrees: "His characters are exact. They're like realities." Bob Tischler, who produced and engineered the *National Lampoon Radio Hour* and four *Lampoon* record albums, who thus has collaborated with much of the top comic talent in the improv business, including Murray and several other Not Ready for Prime Time Players, says simply: "Bill Murray is definitely the most creative improvisational actor I've worked with."

Actually, that last paragraph was a waste of space. It's just an old journalistic tool, the expert testimonial, that allows a writer, under the guise of detached objectivity, to avoid the lifelong burden of critical judgment. In this case it's a waste of space because I figure most people who get to view Murray in action will come to more or less the same conclusion.

Certainly I felt that way about Murray before I got this assignment, but in person he reinforced my thinking in a few ways I wasn't prepared for. The first time I met him, at a bar near NBC called Charley O's, he picked up the check. Don't get any funny ideas, it was the *way* he picked up the check. "Miss?" he called to the waitress, who was standing with her back to us about eight feet away. When she didn't respond, he lunged from his chair and crashed full-length on the floor with a terrible thud, his face at her feet. "Uh, may we have the check please?" he asked the horrified woman.

A few days later we met backstage at NBC in the makeup room a short while before dress rehearsal for the *Saturday Night* hosted by O.J. Simpson. Makeup is not Murray's favorite part of show business. "This is a terrible job," he said. "They put plastic on your face, and then

EDIE BASKIN

they put stuff on that dissolves the plastic. All entertainers end up with skin cancer." Cancer is a minor complaint, however; Murray particularly hates makeup because they keep telling him to shave his mustache for this role or that. It's become a little joke among the cast.

While he shaved, Gilda Radner came up and ran through a bit they were to do called "Looks at Books," a parody book-talk segment hosted by Jane Curtin. With feigned petulance he commented that it was a funny piece, funny for *Gilda,* but why did *he* have to have all the straight lines? He needn't have worried, for when they performed it that evening, he stole it away with an inspired act of bufoonery. (Actually it was cut from the program after the dress rehearsal ran overtime, but Bill and Gilda repeated it two weeks later.) The bit concerned two "nerds," members of the Class of '77, who wrote a book about their classmates' experiences since last summer. And true, Murray's lines were completely straight and consisted of the following, in their entirety:

"Ah, well, there's Scott Kendall, who mowed lawns all summer, and he's now going to junior college in South Dakota."

"Then tell her about Ricki Gale."

"A whole bunch of guys got a driveaway car and went out to California, driving shifts and stuff, they took turns and all they did was stop for gas and stuff."

"Yeah. It's all about us and stuff we do and all the work we did writing the book."

"Thank you, Miss Curtin."

But when it comes to playing nerds, Murray is absolutely brilliant (as is Radner). He combed his hair straight down at the sides, buttoned his shirt at the top and wore his pants

EDIE BASKIN

Top, Bill's Richard Burton hosting W.W. II documentary; left, Bill as a sports fan in Philly; opposite, as Walter Cronkite with Garrett's Idi Amin.

LYNN GOLDSMITH

EDIE BASKIN

up to his chest with the belt buckle unfastened. Then for the whole piece he pounded the arms of his chair, undulated his body like a copulating dog, giggled like a hyena, snorted like a pig and oscillated his belly like a giant imbecile frog. Finally, he inserted the line, "That's so funny it's not even funny. How 'bout a noogy for dat," grabbed Gilda and bopped her on the head. It was funnier than a crutch and to my mind the highlight of the show.

Murray starred in another bit that night, one of his presumptuous, gossipy, flighty-brained showbiz reviews on "Weekend Update" that have become so popular they've added a new expression to the current cocktail circuit: "I'm sorry but that's the way I feel. Now get *outta* here, I mean it." In this review Murray chided Woody Allen for being paranoid, telling him to "grow up" and leave the confines of Elaine's. And then, as if Woody Allen were a sulking three-year-old, he said something like: "I'm sorry if that sounds a little rough, but *you* can take it, Woody . . . Woody," and turning sideways, looking over his shoulder, he pulled out his lower lip with his hand, like a big crybaby pout, and repeated, *"Wwwwoody."* The material itself was funny, but that thing with the lower lip put it right there on the edge of madness.

THE DISCIPLINE THAT BILL Murray applies to his art is evidenced by the lack of discipline he applies to his modest, $300-a-month studio apartment on New York's Upper East Side. One might be tempted to say euphemistically that the place looks lived

LYNN GOLDSMITH

in, but in fact the opposite is true. (I assume he spends most of his time in the *Saturday Night* offices at NBC. He told me later, "They expect you to be around a lot, even if you're not doing that much. It's sort of like a family. It's a lonely place, and you sort of feel you should stay around to share the agony.") There's no TV or stereo in the apartment, Murray unplugged the refrigerator a while back because the noise it made gave him headaches, and he figures he's used the kitchen stove to make maybe seven cups of coffee in five months. I did not ask, but I assumed that the bare double mattress sagging against one wall is what he sleeps on. Placing the mattress near the wall allows him enough floor space to organize his books, papers, toys and clothing in convenient piles.

Further evidence of his artistic discipline soon became apparent, however, as we sat down in the two wooden chairs that constitute his furniture and began the interview. We discussed some impressions he's done on the show—Walter Cronkite, Eric Sevareid and Robert Duvall—and as he spoke his face kept resembling someone I couldn't quite pinpoint.

His explanation of Cronkite began, with uncanny accuracy, in Cronkite's own voice, a hollow, slightly hoarse growl squeezed out in even, staccato bursts, "Itsa-rhythm-that-comes-right-from—" then switched back to Murray's voice. "He's projecting in the back of his throat, and he's not projecting high, so it's bouncing off the front of his throat and then back up and out." Murray laughed. "He may say I'm crazy, but this is how *I* do it."

I asked how Sevareid was different. "Well, they're similar, and when I was doing him I thought, 'Oh God, it sounds like Cronkite, I'm in big trouble here.' But it's just because, I think, they all worked together for so long that they really have picked up each other's business a little bit." Murray then did Sevareid, and while similar, it was perceptibly different, the staccato a bit faster, the voice slightly higher, slowing and sliding off at the end of each phrase: " 'Just - as - you - c'not - teach - old - dogs - new - tricks - so - you - c'not - teach - a - young - generation - of - video - addicts - to - r-e-e-e-a-d.'

And - he - sli-i-i-des. At - the - e-n-n-d. And [Murray popped open his mouth, making a clacking noise with his lips, saliva and tongue] he takes big [*clack*] clackers [*clack*], puckers sort of, you know [*clack*], it's a clack is what it is [*clack*], it's like a horse sound [*clack*], and he does it at the end of his sentences. And he has real good contact, a real strange angle with the cards."

In learning an impression, Murray usually tries to get a tape cassette of the subject and play it over and over, often during cab rides, no doubt creating a different sort of impression in the mind of the cabdriver. "Duvall was one where I really spent a lot of time with a tape recorder in a cab," he continued. "I really enjoyed doing his voice because it's so difficult, there's no hard edges to it. And to get it you really gotta . . . make your brain come through the bottom of your mouth." Bill rolled his eyes and laughed. "Here we go again, watch out. But it was like, when you watch Duvall, the thing that's interesting is his lower lip and the lower half of his mouth. That's where all his meaning comes from, 'cause he's tilting his head, his eyes do a little thing, but the bottom half of his mouth always shows what he's thinking. So if you can make your thinking, like your attitude about it, come through the bottom of your mouth, then you got it. 'Cause his voice is real hard to do. The guy's been all over—I think he's an Army brat—and he's got one of these mysterious voices that has everything in it. It's like. . . ." Murray tilted his head and spoke softly to an imaginary Godfather. " 'What do you want me to do about it? Okay.' It's like, there's a little bit of pain but I'll do anything . . . from the bottom of the mouth."

Yet despite the art and science with which Murray approaches his impressions of the famous, they are not exactly his favorite thing to do. "Impressions really aren't a higher form of life," he confided. "There aren't too many people who make their career by them, and those

who do end up hanging by a noose doing eight different characters as they swing." One might say, in fact, that for Murray life itself is a higher form of impression. Many of the characters he creates are essentially composites of friends or strangers he's observed, of their traits and expressions, sometimes just their attitudes.

His reviewer, for example, is not based on anyone in the business; he's never even seen Rex Reed do a review. "I was doing that character before there were reviewers on TV," he said. "And it was, 'Get *outta* here, you're a *nut,* you're *tremendous* and I *love* ya.' " By now his voice had changed to that soft, effusive, "sweet-sell" quality he uses not only for his reviewer, but to some extent, his TV director and lounge singer. "He's *mad,* he's *insane.* And it's a combination of a few people I've seen who say, 'Hey . . . you're *terrific,* and you

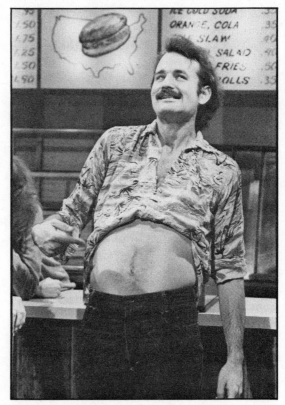

LYNN GOLDSMITH

know it. Hey ... your stuff is *incredible."*

"And there definitely *is* an attitude behind the character. I really hate critics. They're usually wrong, and when they're right, they're right for the wrong reasons. When they do like something, they like it for just *absurd* reasons. Like my first review, I reviewed *The Deep,* and I hated Robert Shaw 'cause I couldn't define his accent. And, you know, 'Nick Nolte, lose the mustache, come on. You look like a Denver cop.' It's like, because they've seen this guy's movie they're on a first-name basis with him. They imply that they know everybody when there are all sorts of people who won't even talk to them and think of them as the sleaziest sort of person."

Murray's remarkable ability to observe, recall and articulate people may be the result of his having always been around so many of them. The fifth of nine children, he was born twenty-seven years ago in Evanston, Illinois, and raised in Wilmette. His father was a lumber salesman who died ten years ago without ever making much money. The kids slept three to a room and during the day were confined to Catholic schools. Bill's only dramatic training consisted of trying to make his father laugh at the dinner table.

When he enrolled as a premed student at Regis College, "a Jesuit play school in Denver," Murray tasted freedom and went nuts. He was a terrible student but quite an accomplished carouser. Mainly, he'd never seen so many different kinds of people. He eventually met even more people in his travels around the country dealing top-grade Jamaican weed by the kilo. For this benevolent service he received more than money; in a sense he got dosed with humanity, and it had a curious side effect: it made him real funny.

"I got so I could tell stories of what I'd done and get laughs," he recalled. "I could tell stories about the time I got arrested in Crook, Colorado, and taken back to Sterling—they'd almost caught me with drugs. And the guy who fingerprinted me knew I had *had* drugs but I'd destroyed 'em somehow, so he's fingerprinting me [Murray began fingerprinting himself on the arm of his chair, brutally pressing down on each finger with his other hand and talking slowly, like a tough old cop]: 'You know, Bill ... just relax ... the toughest thing I ever did ...' and he's *crushing* my finger and being so sweet, he's playing good cop and bad cop at the same time, you know? '... the toughest thing I ever did was cut down ... gimme that other hand ... was cut down a twelve-year-old boy ... who'd hung himself after takin' a fatal dose of L ... S ... D.'

"And I used to do the whole thing, being led across the town square of Sterling, in handcuffs." Here Murray got up and walked to the center of the room, his arms outstretched as if manacled, and I realized I was witnessing a repeat of what had happened years ago—Bill almost subconsciously breaking into performance.

"And this was like prehip, I was one of the first hip dressers, and I had on this cowboy hat [*he adjusts the hat, then puts his hands back in the cuffs*] and one of those real long coats, those army coats, one of the first ones [*starts strutting around the room, his hands out in front*], it was a real strange look and in *this* town it was *bizarre.* So they led me into the Western Union office where I claimed the check for my bail [*signs for the check on the palm of his hand*]. And the guard's got his hand on his hip the whole time [*checks the gun on his hip*], like I'm a dangerous character, and I'm lookin' at all the women [*leers over his shoulder, very cool*], just being a terrorist. ..."

Bill sat down in his chair, stretched and pulled back his hair, and suddenly it came to me who he resembled. I think it was his wistful eyes and five-o'clock shadow. "You look like somebody," I told him.

"Who, Irwin Corey?"

True, he does look like the nutty professor, but I was thinking about someone else. "No," I said, "Emmett Kelly."

ON HIS TWENTY-FIRST BIRTH-day, Bill Murray gazed at the world around him and discovered he was in jail. He'd been busted at the Chicago airport with eight and a half pounds of grass. Actually, the cops weren't looking for drugs, they were looking for bombs. Murray had tried to get a TWA flight with his "under twenty-one" card, was turned down for lack of an ID and had remarked petulantly, "That's too bad, I wanted to get on 'cause I got two bombs in my suitcase." He tried to stow the bags in a locker, but he had no change and they caught him. "It was stupid, but I guess I was turning myself in," said Bill. "But I did do one good thing: I ate a check this guy had given me that was in the suitcase, and that guy owes me his life and reputation." [That man was Arnold Beresford, a second-grade teacher at Our Lady of the Sea girls' school, Des Moines.]

The bust made the front page of the *Chicago Tribune*. Murray was convicted, put on probation and eventually on the street without a job. Meanwhile, an older brother, Brian Doyle-Murray (he changed his name to avoid legal confusion with British actor Brian Murray), had been working as an improv artist for Second City, and Bill felt desperate enough to audition himself. He won a scholarship to study with the Second City workshop and eventually inherited Brian's old parts with the group's road company. Later, he followed in his brother's footsteps to New York, the *National Lampoon Radio Hour* and the *Lampoon*'s off-Broadway revue. The revue played four months, and during that time Bill was seen by Howard Cosell, who immediately hired him for *his Saturday Night Live* on ABC, and by Lorne Michaels, who hired him a year later for *his* on NBC. (Just this year Michaels hired Brian Doyle-Murray as a writer.)

Ironically, Murray's television exposure has begun to interfere somewhat with his practice of observing people; people tend to stare back and it gets embarrassing. So every now and then he tries to walk around spots like 42nd Street and the Lower East Side, where he is less readily recognized and where the material is generally better. It's the sort of thing that keeps Murray going. As he explains: "That's all there is—men, women and animals. And you can't always do animal humor. You got to get into that human stuff."

Hey maniacs, isn't that the truth. Because let's face it, there's a lot of comedians out there who are so funny, they're not even funny. I'm talking to *you,* David Brenner—when are you gonna get off the fucking plane with those airline jokes? "Blue water in the toilet! Blue water in the toilet!"—you think that's funny? Hey, baby, change flights, the laughs got off in Chicago.

Because when it comes to funny, when it comes to mad, when it comes to sleight-of-mind-falling-down-rolling-in-the-aisles genius —hey, Bill Murray, you lunatic leprechaun; you just keep nursing your crock of comedy gold the way you've been doing. *You* tell the world when to say "gotcha!" But one thing, Billy: lose the mustache. Was Tom Dewey funny? Hell no. He lost. So did Pancho Villa. I'm sorry if that sounds rough, but that's the way I feel. Now get *outta* here, I mean it.

EDIE BASKIN

JANE Curtin

DOES NOT GIVE INTERVIEWS

BIRTHPLACE : Cambridge, Massachusetts
BIRTHDATE : September 6th
HEIGHT : 5′5½″
WEIGHT : 124 pounds
HAIR : Light brown
EYES : Gray
RESIDENCE : New York City
PREVIOUS EXPERIENCE : The Proposition improvisational theater group; on tour with "The Last of the Red Hot Lovers"; coauthor of and performer in "Pretzels," an off-Broadway comedy revue.

EDIE BASKIN

GARRETT
Morris

BY FRANK ROSE

IF YOU'RE A FREQUENT VIEWER, you've probably noticed that, of the seven regulars on *Saturday Night Live,* only Garrett Morris has kinky hair and black skin. Millions of other Americans have certainly noticed this remarkable fact. They write him letters about it every week. Gar-

rett told me about these letters recently—got quite animated about them, too. " 'YOU'RE THE ONLY BLACK, HOW DO YOU FEEL? YOU'RE THE ONLY BLACK, HOW DO YOU FEEL?' " he shouted. "Oh, my God! I mean, it's *obvious* I'm the only black, so where do we go from there? *Laverne and Shirley, Mary Tyler Moore*—my God, 99.44 percent of 'em do not have *anybody* black there. So I think instead of dealing with this show as having one black person, they ought to write to those shows that have none and say, 'THERE ARE NO BLACKS! HOW DO YOU FEEL ABOUT THAT?' "

We were sitting in the office

RAIN WORTHINGTON

EDIE BASKIN

Garrett shares with writer Alan Zweibel on the uptown side of the RCA Building, seventeen floors above the street. Garrett was wearing a Cosmos jersey, faded jeans, gray socks with a wad of bills stuffed in beside one ankle, and polished black shoes. A dark-skinned boy, naked except for an enormous shell necklace, gazed out at us from a cover of *Natural History* magazine pinned to his bulletin board. "That's me as a kid," he said. A copy of James Jones's *Whistle* lay nearby, masquerading in a phoney book jacket as *Bad Stuff 'Bout the Mets,* by Chico Esquela—Esquela being the Puerto Rican baseball hero who has become Garrett's most unforgettable *Saturday Night* character. I'd caught Garrett in the midst of a long break toward the end of 1978-79 season so the panic that normally grips this place was distinctly absent. While most of the other *Saturday Night* people went on vacation, Garrett stayed in New York, tying up some business ends and renovating his Harlem apartment.

I asked if anything had changed, racewise, in the four years since *Saturday Night* had first gone on the air. Just one thing, he replied, and that was something he'd vowed to change from the start: about the middle of the fourth season, the writers finally began putting him in situations where he didn't have to eat ham hocks and collard greens or hail from the West Indies. In other words, they began to conceive of him as one of the group instead of as the group's representative black person. "Some people think it's unnatural to do that," he said. "Okay. John is Albanian. Why not then do everything he does as Albanian? Everything Gilda does should be Jewish. Everything Bill does should be Irish. *Then I'm cool.* But don't tell me that all I've gotta do is be black and everybody else has got a racial background you can't see—why? because they're white.

"Most white Jewish writers think they know everything," he continued. "That's right, they do! They figure they know every-*thing!* If you're black and you come in and say, 'Look, a black may not say that,' they know that you're wrong because they've heard one black dude say this, right? So I've had to deal with the *enormous* volume of white Jewish ego. Hey, here's a white Jewish guy right now. Hello, Alan, how ya doin'?"

Zweibel dropped a parcel on his desk and grinned. "I was just in the area, figured I'd drop in. How ya doin', man?"

"Uh, I need some advice on a monologue. You know, like when I go in front of these . . . white groups in Oregon. Two blacks in the whole town, right?" A couple of weeks before, Garrett had made his debut as a public speaker at a tiny college in McMinnville, Oregon.

"How'd it go?" Alan asked.

"I had 'em for about 20, 25 minutes. Then I started saying, 'Hey, I hear that Pushkin was black. I hear that Beethoven might have been black. By that ratio, since we now don't even relate to Pushkin or Beethoven as anything but

JEFFREY SWITZER

Opposite, top: Garrett as Tina Turner with backup singers Gilda, Jane & Laraine; bottom, as Alex Haley in "Roots"; this page, Sammy Davis, Jr. (Garrett) & Peter Lawford (Bill) with Dolly Parton (Jane) in sketch on celebrity fundraisers.

white, in about sixty or seventy years, Duke *Ellington'*ll be white.' They didn't laugh, you know what I mean?"

Alan thought for a second, then said, "Maybe the way to go with that is to take some black guy whom you really can't stand and everybody thinks is an asshole and say he wasn't black. Take some real dipshit. Say Sammy Davis is white. Take all the good white guys and say they were black and then take one black guy who's an asshole and say he was white. I don't have any of 'em here, I have 'em at home, but I have about 1100 jokes. In fact, those are the jokes I auditioned for Lorne with four years ago. Some of them are black-like things and maybe we can update 'em. I'll bring 'em in."

After Alan had left, I asked Garrett what the people who write in think about his being the only black. His response was impatient. "They think basically the same thing everybody else

thinks," he said. "That there must be some- thing strange. What I'm saying is that there have been problems with the racial thing, but that's *no surprise!*

"I was born in New Orleans in 1937. Here I am at NBC in 1979, and I've gone from a totally segregated society to one that's sup- posedly desegregated but which, in a very short period of time, I find out is just as cutting. Look, we gonna *die* with something racial being in my head, man. I mean there's no way around it. To me, it's a part of *American life.* In 1975, I could leave *Saturday Night Live* and I'd be there from one o'clock until two o'clock trying to catch a cab. So there I was, a TV 'star,' in quotations, and I couldn't catch a cab—just because I was pointin' my thumb uptown, and black. Right now there's a cab company that has an account with my company and with NBC and it's like pulling teeth to get the guys to come uptown to pick me up. Man, you'd be

Left, "Amy Bedtime" with Amy Carter (Sissy Spacek) and nanny (Garrett); opposite, Garrett in a sketch on his ancestor Boto, who's at the root of the Morris family tree.

EDIE BASKIN

EDIE BASKIN

in Bellevue if you was to be dealing with this shit every day like it was serious. You know, fuck that."

THERE IS A SKIT CALLED "CARD

Game" in *Saturday Night* #25 that says a great deal about the Garrett Morris experience without seeming to say much about it at all. The skit features Danny Aykroyd as a nineteenth-century New Orleans gentleman; Garrett Morris as his shuffling manservant, Johnny Sackpants; Chevy Chase as Mr. Dierga, the greatest card player of all Europe; and Elliot Gould as Dierga's interpreter and backer, Mo Greenstein. While Greenstein keeps up a constant chatter about Southern hospitality and their

honor as gentlemen, Dierga deals out a very strange game of five-card draw punctuated by staccato bursts of nonsense Spanish. First he deals five cards to his host and keeps the rest of the deck for himself; then he transfers random stacks of gold from his host's pile to his own; finally he reaches across the table and looks at his host's hand. ("You don't play dealer's look in this country?" Greenstein inquires innocently.) Sackpants looks on aghast as his master is taken in by this blatant hustle. Finally, unable to contain himself, he says, "Mr. Russo, man, he is *bustin' yo' chops!*" Mr. Russo brushes him aside, however, letting Dierga and Greenstein make their exit with all the stakes in their pockets and two golden candlelabra under their arms. Sackpants knows better than to say anything more. He is a negro who *knows his place,* as they used to say down South.

When he was eleven years old and living with his grandfather in Morgan City, Louisiana, 75 miles west of New Orleans on the Atchafalaya River, Garrett Morris got in a fight with a white guy who was stupider than he. That was a bad mistake. Garrett had gotten caught in the chain of a bicycle he'd been told to ride by the white man, who was his boss. He told the white man the bike needed a guard, but the white man said it didn't. He insisted it did, and—well, you can just imagine the rest. The white guy took a punch at him, and Garrett swung back, and somebody called the police, and the police were just about ready to rearrange Garrett's uppity black features when his grandfather came in and sweet-talked him out of there. His grandfather was a Baptist preacher, which Garrett figures is the only thing that saved him.

Like he said, Garrett Morris was born in New Orleans in 1937. His father was in the Navy and his mother decided she could make better money as a hairdresser in Houston, so he was left in New Orleans for relatives to raise. He lived with some aunts in Gert Town until

EDIE BASKIN

he was five—Gert Town, that's a colored section in back of Xavier U.; then he was sent to Morgan City to live with his grandparents until he was about thirteen; then he came back to New Orleans and lived in Backa Town—Backa Town, that's a colored section in back of the French Quarter—with some folks on his father's side while he went to Booker T. Washington High. After high school he went to Dillard University on Gentilly Boulevard and majored in music. After that he went North.

The central fact about Garrett Morris is that he is a black man who came of age in New Orleans in the early 1950s. From that, everything else derives: the early career as a singer of classical music; the visceral response to Malcolm X and other black leaders of the sixties;

the ensuing career as an actor, comedic and otherwise; and the lingering *thing* he has about the ultimate taboo, that unnatural impulse, that carnal crime, the one they rail against, and preach about and chop your nuts off for (if you're black; otherwise, never mind). I'm talking about mongrelization of the races.

"If you come from New Orleans and you're alive," he said that afternoon in his office, "nothing can fuck with you. The racism was—you couldn't even cut it, you had to chip at it. You just fix your mind a certain way and after a few years you can deal with it. White women, for instance, were not there. They just were not there. Your dick didn't get hard, because if your dick got hard you might not have a dick. You knew the swimming holes to go to—the worst ones. Your place was near the tracks or the coal chute, where there was the most noise and the most pollution. You knew the white part of town. Nobody had to tell you, you'd just be walking and suddenly you'd see—aw, *pavement* here! Wherever it was near the river and you could sit—no, you didn't go there. Except as a servant. And if you knew anybody white, you deferred to 'em. You said 'sir' or you just stepped out of the way. The one or two who might not have done that got either their teeth knocked out or killed. That is the truth, that's God's honest truth.

"And everybody was involved in the most orgiastic religious stuff, whites *and* blacks. And it's just the most peculiar mixture of everything. Man, you go to a Baptist's house and you'll see a Bible, right? Then you'll see a Catholic artifact—the cross. Then you'll see some snakeskin or some gris-gris or some goupa dust around the house. And the food personifies that because Creole cooking, that's what that is—it's a mixing-up of everything.

"Then to have sometimes the same people violate not only the rules of the Christian church but the announced rules of the racial overgroup, right? All this time they're tellin'

EDIE BASKIN

Opposite: Conehead Merkon (Garrett) shares a few packs of cigarettes with Beldar (Dan); this page, left, Garrett with Julian Bond on "Black Perspective"; below, singing Schubert's "An Die Musik."

you how unnatural it is, and somethin' inside me says, 'Damn, if it's unnatural, it ain't gonna happen.' But you're seeing brothers and sisters, one as dark as me and one nearly as light as you, sometimes in the same household, sometimes split up, sometimes not talking to each other. You've grown up in this shit. To see things like this in the community—spotted babies with green eyes, blue eyes, and to still talk about the unnaturalness—and you are a child evolving and all this shit is bombarding you—man, let me tell you ... I don't even know what to say, man, I mean—I'm *lucky*. I'm gonna tell you right now, I'm *lucky*. 'Cause it is ... a *seductive thing*. It beguiles you. You know what I'm talking about? I don't care how well your mother or your father try to protect you, it's some sensuous shit goin' on out there. You'll dip in it and dip in it and dip in it—I mean it's like what you say about how people become juvenile delinquents, but I'm talking about becoming ... a *crazy nigger!*

"The potpourri, which is a New Orleans word, man, jambalaya ... It fed a lot of fan-

EDIE BASKIN

Opposite: Garrett as Johnny Sackpants watches as his master, Mr. Russo (Dan) is hustled by Mr. Dierga (Chevy) & advisor Mo Greenstein (Elliott Gould).

RAIN WORTHINGTON

tasies, it fed a lot of things that were dangerous and eminently sensual. You've got the confusion of race, sex, religion—that has got to begin a slow twisting of your natural impulses. So you may be devil-may-care, you may be a fool, you may be the New Messiah and try to deal with that shit. Otherwise, you better leave town.

"And amid this whole thing is a whole stratification of niggers by niggers into about ten colors or so, which if you're on the light side of that you're cool and if you're on the dark side you're cool if you're achieving something. And the amount of stamina and energy that you're going to see a dark-skinned—a *black,* especially in New Orleans—exhibiting toward this or that social position is almost in inverse proportion to how dark his skin was. If you were dark-skinned, instead of a light-skinned *negro,* many times this would infuse in you a desire to achieve and to overcome it—to be the

best basketball player, to be the best drummer, to be first in whatever it was. In my case it was drama and the choir. Classical music as a thing that was respected in that society became something that could shoot me out where I could have more mobility so I could deal with whoever I wanted to deal with. And at the same time, my sexual energy was going into, shall we say, some of the more perverted areas, which I will not mention here."

Suddenly, Garrett burst into song:

> *Masturbation, it's funny*
> *It makes a cloudy day sunny*
> *That's when I think of you honey*
> *When I masturba-a-ate . . .*

"I mean, look, have you ever read *Portnoy's Complaint?* That's me.

"But I always fantasized about three things," he went on. "Acting, writing, and being involved in music—not just as a singer, but as a writer, too. I always fantasized about that, I can't remember when I didn't. I don't know if I ever really questioned it. And it wasn't some great calling kind-of-thing, it was just that that was always what I thought about doing."

OF THE NUMEROUS MUSICAL

skits Morris has done for *Saturday Night Live,* two are especially memorable. One is his breathless portrayal of Tina Turner singing "Proud Mary" on show #82: Clad in a monstrous red wig and a slinky orange-spangled dress that stops at the hips, he churns out the saga of a hapless bunny rabbit who gets his ears caught in the millwheel and ends up looking like tomato bisque. (Michael O'Donoghue's Mr. Mike, as the other half of the Mike & Tina Turner Revue, having altered the story somewhat). He got a lot of letters about his legs after that one. The other, on show #118, was a little more sedate. He dressed regular, and the number he sang was Schubert's "An Die Musik." As he performed, the following crawl appeared on TV screens across the nation:

"Guess we owe you an explanation. Garrett came up to the office several weeks ago and said, 'I'd like to sing on the show. I want to do an old favorite of mine.' So we figured, great, he'll do 'Sunny,' he'll do 'Devil with the Blue Dress On,' he'll do 'Boogaloo Down Broadway,' But no, he comes in with Schubert's 'An Die Musik.' What could we say? What would you do in our position? Tell him. 'Garrett, it's too middle-class?' No. You'd do what we did. You'd be polite. You'd realize there's nothing wrong with doing this kind of thing. I mean, frankly, we're *tired* of being thought of as just a comedy show when we *know* we can do so much more. And besides, who was going to tell him? He carries a knife. . . ."

As a little boy growing up in Morgan City, Louisiana, Garrett Morris often listened to classical music at his grandfather's knee. This may seem odd but it makes a certain kind of sense

when you think about it. After all, the white man could tell black folks to keep their hands off his women, and their kids out of his schools, and their asses out of his neighborhood, but he couldn't tell them not to tune into the *Bell Telephone Hour* on the radio every week. And since the white man always had what was best, and since this music is the culmination of one thousand years of white musical achievement, it had to be good, right? Of course, Garrett learned gospel music at his grandfather's knee too, and he sang it in his grandfather's choir. But gospel is a vernacular form; if you're serious about music, you have to operate on their terms. You did then, anyway.

In 1957, Garrett's music teacher at Dillard brought him North to study conducting at Tanglewood. He returned to New Orleans to graduate ("not *summa cum laude,* not *magna cum laude:* I graduated 'thank you lawdy'"), then moved to New York, settled into the YMCA on 125th Street in Harlem, and started studying at Juilliard. He passed an audition not long after that and became a part-time chorus singer for the Harry Belafonte Singers; he toured and recorded with Belafonte for years after that doing everything from rock to folk to classical to semi-classical. By 1960 he had married a soprano, moved to the Bronx, and switched to the Manhattan School of Music. He was drafted into the Army in 1961, but a year and a half later he was bounced out after offering to punch his sergeant, who was white and Southern. This incident convinced his commanding officer that Garrett was too crazy to keep in the stockade so the Army got rid of him on an obscure regulation, permitting early discharge for men with seasonal occupations. Designed primarily to help farmboys at harvest time, it was applied in Garrett's case after he got a letter requesting his services as assistant conductor for a spring concert series.

In the mid-sixties, Garrett's marriage and

career began to stagnate simultaneously. He dealt with the former by moving into another Y, with the latter by putting music aside. By that time he'd ceased being a hot young talent-on-the-rise and had became one of those geniuses whose gifts go unappreciated. Then Malcolm X said "Fuck Whitey," and "it was either that or I was gonna fail the courses anyway.

"But a lot of the ideas that Malcolm X expressed solidified something in my head about classical music that had been bugging me," he said. "I just started paying more attention to *black* infiltrations—you know, idioms—and for a little while I thought that I, too, had forsaken my roots. Which I had, in the sense of—I mean, I could *never* not sing what I had learned as a kid at my grandfather's feet. But I knew there had to be some way to deal with what I had learned as a kid in terms as eloquent as I was dealing with classical music. And I didn't want to do that. I said, 'Now's a good time to check out acting.' "

Within a year, Garrett had broken all ties to the music business and set out to make it as an actor and a playwright. For the next decade he lived the marginal existence one associates with the theater while enjoying enough success to make it all look promising. Several of his plays got produced, including a children's show about the downfall of a corrupt ice cream mogul ("awful," he said) and a serious work about a black cop's indentity crisis during the racial uprisings of the Sixties. He appeared on Broadway in *The Great White Hope* and *Ain't Supposed To Die a Natural Death* among others and was a regular on an ABC-TV series called *Roll-out* which was cancelled halfway into the season. He acted in various movies, including *Where's Poppa?, The Anderson Tapes,* and *Cooley High.* Then, despite his inexperience in comedy, he was hired by producer Lorne Michaels as an apprentice writer for *Saturday Night Live.*

Lorne claims he wasn't looking for a black writer specifically; in fact, he's not even sure he knew Garrett was black before they met. He'd gone to the Writers Guild, a union of professional writers for radio, television, and the movies, for help in setting up an apprentice program because his initial budget at NBC allowed for only four fulltime writers. Garrett was recommended by then-deputy executive director Elihu Winer on the basis of his plays, some of which had comedic aspects. Lorne was impressed enough to hire him, and after he saw his performance in *Cooley High,* he was impressed enough to make him one of his Not Ready for Prime Time Players.

Garrett's background as an actor and a singer has consistently set him apart from the other performers on *Saturday Night Live,* most of whom came to the show from *National Lampoon* productions and improvisational comedy troupes. He continues to think of himself as an actor rather than a comedian, and unlike, say John Belushi and Gilda Radner, he does not go in much for slapstick or broad caricatures. After three and a half seasons, though Garrett finally got his shot with Chico Esquela. Chico was created by Brian Doyle-Murray (Bill's older brother and *SNL* writer) in a skit about a former All-Star second baseman who is engaged to speak at a Knights of Columbus banquet but proves unable to say more than a dozen words in English. About the only thing he can say, in fact, is "Baseball been bery, bery good to me" and "Keep your eye on de ball." Alan Zweibel, the writer in charge of "Weekend Update," liked Garrett's performance so much he got together with Murray and decided to make Chico a Jim Bouten-type sportscaster. Hence, Chico's *Bad Stuff 'Bout the Mets* book, his short-lived comeback attempt, and his return to "Weekend Update" with the choice observation that "News been bery, bery good to me."

Chico has captured the public like nothing else Garrett has done on the show. Teenagers run up to him on the street to get his auto-

EDIE BASKIN

graph. People write him letters that don't ask how it feels to be the only black. And everywhere he goes, people call him by that strange Spanish name that means Chico School. Yet one of the things that's so remarkable about Chico School is that he had to wait so long to be developed.

"Saturday Night Live has been an experience that, you know . . . it hasn't been all right," he said. "Everybody here hasn't been all right, including myself, every time. And there've been a lot of times–one or two times–when I did say the words "I quit" and mean it and walk out. Patience is what I needed, and that's what I got out of it. It's a great group of people to work with–there's so much talent and brilliance around." He lowered his voice, almost to a whisper. "Sometimes it's dazzling." More than that he would not say.

ONE OF GARRETT'S FAVORITE skits is one that aired on show #16. It opens with a conservatively-dressed Garrett Morris sitting behind a desk, announcing that he wants to talk to "all you white Americans about the way black people have been treated" in this country. "I know a lot of you feel guilty," he continues, "and you should. My great-great-grandmother was brought over here on a slave ship and raped by her white master. And my grandfather was lynched by a mob for not tipping his hat to a white lady. Now, there's nothing you can do to relieve their suffering. However, if you would like to relieve your guilt, I am willing to accept money as a representative of four hundred years of oppression. Send cash or money order to: White Guilt Relief Fund. . . ."

If Garrett's real-life hustles lack the verve of the White Guilt Relief Fund, they nonetheless have a certain zing of their own. Take his plans for an elegant black skin magazine to be called *Storyville,* which he described as "a New Or-

leans-decadent-sexual-racial-philosophical-psychological-Third-World magazine." Besides trying to show up *Playboy* and *Penthouse* as rich men's mags, he said, *Storyville* will "try to have us understand that literacy can dwell in the same place as does the raunch and that, in fact, even the popes have been guilty of having hard dicks and that didn't stop them from being whatever they were. That to be a sensuous person, to be a passionate person, is healthy, is right, is good. That it should be out in the world, you know. That it is wrong that you should read in the *New York Times* everything you want, from the most superficial bullshit to the most violent stuff, including pictures of Vietnamese with their guts hanging out, and never see a dick and a pussy.

"It's got to get to where it's the whole person that's being dealt with. To me, that is critical. That is one of the purposes of sex magazines that has not been dealt with. Larry Flynt has tried to deal with it in another way, but he's been too shocking to achieve that end. *Playboy* brushes out the pussy, so we know that they've got to have some guilt or something about sex. But there's a way in which New Orleans decadence, French decadence, describes what I mean. Oscar Wilde time, right? Casanova. Flaubert. Cleopatra, that kind of thing. Cleopatra, I understand was a *bona fide* fellatrice. Look, the whole of Greco-Roman culture probably *hangs* on her *mouth!* You understand what I'm saying?

"I think that whatever was happening in politics and in race, particularly in the sixties, got bogged up because of a whole distorted view of sex. Now, in the South, the white bigots were saying, 'Well, it's mongrelization,' and while all that's happening the black militants were saying something that's not necessarily as way out, but what's implied is, you can deal with the whole spectrum of black color– which is really fantastic, man, I can deal with the darkest to the very lightest and still be gettin' away clean, you know what I mean?—but don't let her be really white. But it seems to me that if you say the black mind is free, then you have to deal with the possibility of that. It ain't really free unless that possibility is there and no ostracism comes out of it. Then you have the ideal situation.

"I'm very much an idealist in that way. It has nothing to do with my intentions, with my wanting that. But nobody can tell you who to go to bed with at night. When you close the door at night, you want to be with somebody you really want to be with, and it may not be somebody of your race. It may be somebody from Outer Mongolia, you know, who really *understands* your shit."

It probably bears mentioning that for the past two years, Morris has been living with a black woman.

"But if you look at her," he said, "you might see that the white man did mess around with the black maids and shit. But see, that's another thing—because as dark as I am, or as white as you are, it is possible that you could go back in your history and see something that you didn't expect to be there. What I'm saying is that none of us know anything, man.

"And yet it is true about Pushkin. Pushkin woulda had to sit in the back of the bus in 1945 in Mississippi. According to our social definition of a negro, Pushkin was a negro. Beethoven? Check out Beethoven, that's all I'm saying. I dare anyone who's reading this to disprove it. When Beethoven was a kid, his friends described him as having black-brownish skin. Now, do you know any white men who are described as having black-brownish skin? I'm saying to you that Beethoven was referred to by the French emperor as "my blackamoor." Now, Spain was much whiter prior to the

Moors, right? I think it was like his great-great-grandparents hooked up with a Moor, right? Then I think one generation stayed there in Spain, then they went to Holland, and finally they got to Leipzig. Out comes Beethoven, who was always listening to Spanish music in the background, if you know what I mean. And Beethoven was an innovator. The seventh, which is very important to jazz, was a contribution of Beethoven's. Wa-da-da-*daaaa*—that note there, that wasn't in music the way Beethoven used it until he came along. So just dig that. If I'm proved wrong by anybody reading ROLLING STONE, I'll give them a thousand fucking dollars. Put up or shut up. That's what I'm saying.

"Well, now, why was it important whether he was black or white? Check it out: I got all the white images I need here in America. I coulda used *one* black up there doing *something*. There's no way for me to deal with 'why was it important?' I don't wanna hear that shit. The truth is important. Maybe I woulda had ten years wiped outta my struggle to do something in music, had I been given that."

As it happens, Garrett has recently returned to his struggle in music. He's writing a ballet with lyrics that are the Greek prayer, *Kyrie Eleison.* "I'm trying to work out the form according to, you know, exposition, development, recapitulation," he explained, "but with the insides being jazz, rock and roll, classical all mixed together as well as I can do it. So it's ballet that is, in fact, the *Kyrie Eleison,* with a soprano solo, a classical chorus, a brass band, a rhythm section." I had a sudden vision of his ballet as a creole jambalaya, a still life of Bible, crucifix, and gris-gris, a spotted baby with green eyes. "We'll see what happens, you know?"

EDIE BASKIN

JOHN
Belushi

(1949-1992)

BY CHARLES M. YOUNG

I FEEL REALLY WEIRD OPENING up my personal life this way," says John Belushi. "But what is there to see? Just a lot of old boxes." Hoisting one on my shoulder, I walk downstairs from his Greenwich Village apartment and dump it in the trunk of the Bluesmobile, a 1967 Dodge Monaco with a fresh coat of jet-black paint. Belushi has discovered a unique way of making reporters useful: if they must ask nosy questions, the least they can do is save you some bucks in moving expenses. Actually, there is more to see in the apartment than old boxes—enormous piles of dirty clothes, two Persian cats, an autographed picture of Ray Charles—but the day is hot, my wind short and my eye for the revealing detail concomitantly dull. As if to reward my efforts, he selects a revealing detail for me.

"They'd just shot me up with morphine," he says, indicating a

RAIN WORTHINGTON

Left, John as Pete, Greek restaurant owner; below, as Lou Grant to Laraine's Mary Tyler Moore and Steve Martin's Ted Baxter in "Mary's Dead"; opposite: Samurai Night Fever.

photograph of himself as a dazed cowboy on the set of *Goin' South,* one of three movies Belushi acted in during the past year, in addition to twenty *Saturday Night Live* shows. "A squib exploded in my hand. We were in Mexico, so they just picked out the splinters and shot me up and we went on with the scene."

Did the morphine affect his acting ability?

"I don't know. It was just a gunfight. . . . I think it'll be a great movie. It has Indians, Mexicans, Orientals, gold, railroads, barroom brawls, bank robberies, horse stealing, everything a Western should have—but no heavy violence."

Dressed in army fatigues and a white T-shirt, Belushi looks capable of handling any sort of violence. Or starting it. His face gives the permanent impression of demented anger lurking barely beneath the surface—an impression reinforced by an incipient beard (now that he is off *Saturday Night* for the summer) and a potbelly of the sort usually associated with redneck sheriffs. When he plays the samurai or the crazy weatherman on TV, the effect is

EDIE BASKIN

hilarious, but up close it's disconcerting. I've known the guy for over a year and have never been quite sure he wasn't about to crush my knees with a brick.

THE SAME VIOLENT URGE THAT makes John great will also ultimately destroy him," says Michael O'Donoghue, a *National Lampoon* alumnus and writer for three seasons on *Saturday Night Live.* O'Donoghue's humor is best exemplified by his infamous imitation of Tony Orlando and Dawn with needles poked in their eyes. He expects *SNL* to fall into "the enema bank" without him to keep the show in the mainstream of American humor.

"I appeared with John and Steve Allen once on *Midday Live* (a local New York talk pro-gram hosted by Bill Boggs)," O'Donoghue continues. "Boggs kept asking him to do an Elvis Presley imitation, and I knew John had no ending for it. Finally he agreed, and to get out of the bit, he picked up a glass of water, threw it at Boggs, hit him in the chest and knocked over a table full of plants. You should have seen Steve Allen's face. It turned into the Hollywood Wax Museum. I don't see John ever becoming that stable. He's one-hundred percent Albanian, you know, the only one you're ever likely to meet. I tell him Albanians are gypsies whose wagons broke down. I have this vision of him with a goose under his arm, trying to sneak out of the room. Yes, that is John: an Albanian goose thief.

"He's one of those hysterical personalities that will never be complete. I look for him to

EDIE BASKIN

end up floating dead after the party. Comedy is a baby seal hunt."

Sitting in the backyard of

Belushi's new apartment after we have moved a Bluesmobile full of boxes into storage in the basement, Belushi counts the steps on the stairway to his second-floor balcony. He is pleased to discover they number thirteen, the same as on the gallows where he tries to hang Jack Nicholson in *Goin' South.* The huge new apartment has two floors and a chandeliered living room—highly suitable for a television star on the verge of almost certain movie stardom in the coming year. Maybe even the coming month, with *Animal House,* a comedy premiering in New York City, July 28th, 1978, and scheduled for release in 400 theaters by the middle of August. Universal is counting on a hit, having budgeted about $3.5 million for promotion (the movie itself cost $2.8 million). Their faith is well placed. *Animal House* is hilarious. Written by Douglas Kenney and Chris Miller of the *National Lampoon* and Harold Ramis, formerly of *Playboy,* the movie has much the same sensibility that made the *Lampoon*'s high-school yearbook such a hit. The product of people in their midtwenties to early thirties, the film relays a message from a generation that marched against the war and held gross-out contests to a generation that gets congratulated in *U.S News and World Report* for shutting up and attending medical school: trash something, people, or you won't have anything to remember at your five-year reunion.

"I've seen *Animal House* two and a half times now at sneak previews with a real audience, and the reaction was great," says Belushi. "Your face ends up forty feet high and if you blow a line during the filming, you can just do it again. If you blow it on TV, it's gone forever. But I want to continue doing both next season. After that, I don't know."

Belushi's schedule this past season was overwhelming. On Sundays after the TV show, he flew to location (Durango, Mexico, for *Goin' South;* Eugene, Oregon, for *Animal House;* and Los Angeles for *Old Boyfriends)* and flew back on Thursdays for *Saturday Night Live* rehearsals. Because three days of stubble was required for two of the movies and outlawed on the show, just keeping his shaving schedule straight was complicated enough, let alone learning his lines. To keep his life together under such circumstances, I suggest, he must be on a more even keel than he was during the first two years of the show.

"Those were very hard times . . . uh . . . very tough, dealing with fame and success, while trying to fulfill your responsibility to the audience," he says. "The trick is knowing what you want to do and then resolving to do everything you have to do to get there."

Does that mean his self-destructive tendencies are under control?

"I think it . . . uh . . . I don't know. It comes along with a certain kind of lifestyle, which you don't change after becoming well known. Everything becomes more heightened, takes on more urgency, and the tendency to self-destruct heightens too. I'm learning to cope and not deny my own success, but I still think it's not happening a lot. I get nervous, and I am capable of doing something to blow it on purpose. A lot of actors have that problem."

John Belushi is not your

basic great quote. He tends to not finish sentences before moving on to the next thought. He tends to say things like, "The sky is blue," and then five minutes later say, "Uh, let's put that sky-is-blue stuff off the record. It might offend my fans in Brooklyn," leaving the impression his career will be over, his wife will divorce him, and his cats eaten by wild dogs if you don't put your pen down. That's if he likes you. Once, a double-knit TV reporter wearing white shoes got him to sit down on the set of *Animal House* for an interview and asked how it was to work in movies, as opposed to live television. Belushi paused for a moment, shot him an I'll-eat-your-kneecaps-for-breakfast look and asked, "How much do you make, anyway?"

Furthermore, when John Belushi bothers to be funny around reporters, much of the humor depends on him breaking into weird accents at unexpected moments. Black letters on white paper just cannot convey the humor of his Greek restaurant character suddenly showing up next to you in an airplane seat to Los Angeles and demanding, "Shut door! City of New York don't pay me to air-condition streets! What you want? We have very good strawberry pie. You just want grilled cheese? You cheap bastard!"

Nor is Belushi much given to self-analysis. One of his great imitations is of Joe Cocker, the English R&B singer with the stage mannerisms of a cerebral palsy victim. *Saturday Night Live* fans usually do not remember individual sketches that well, but everyone remembers the night Belushi sang a duet with Cocker. For some it was hilarious, for others, it was cruel. Belushi himself won't even watch the tape. "It was all rehearsed," he says. "So I asked him to do it a long time before. It was just, uh . . . the answer . . . uh . . . I don't know why I did it. It was very emotional. Don't ask me why I did it."

All of this is to John Belushi's long-term advantage. He has as strong a sense of his own emotional integrity as anyone I have ever met. Some part of his mind is simply inviolable, and as long as he is in the public eye, people will want to know what John Belushi is *really* like. And John Belushi won't tell them.

In pursuit of the impossible dream, then, let us consider some biographical facts.

John Belushi was born January 24th, 1949.

He is one-hundred-percent Albanian, which he refuses to discuss. (Belushi expressed great dismay when I told him I'd been planning to use his Albanian heritage as a humorous motif in this profile. Since he is an expert in both comedy and imitating people with strange accents, I took his word that his ancestral homeland is not funny.) He seems to have been a nightmare to his schoolteachers. In the sixth grade, they demoted him to second grade to sober him out of his antics. Also in the sixth grade, his gym teacher announced in front of his class that he was the worst of her 400 students and kicked him in the balls. "They crushed the spirit out of me by the time I left," he insists.

Attending Wheaton, Illinois, Central High School, he acquired the nickname Wrestling Shoes from his cousins. "They were a couple of years older and much funnier than me," he recalls. "Every time I opened my mouth, they would cut me down. We were playing poker one New Year's Eve, and they won all my money. I left the table and suddenly burst into tears. They asked me what was wrong, and I said, 'That was for my wrestling shoes.' So they called me Wrestling Shoes ever after."

Bored by his classes, Belushi expended most of his energies playing drums in rock bands, acting in school shows and being captain of the football team. They were conference champions his junior year and finished in a tie for second place the following year. "I must have been the laziest captain they ever had," he says. "I was kicked off the team every year for loafing. The coach used to yell at us to do something or turn in our uniforms. If I felt I'd already done my best, I'd just run to the locker room and turn in my uniform. But I was always back the next day. I never missed a practice. It was a very valuable experience. After two-a-day practices at the end of summer, you feel there's nothing you can't do. I probably wouldn't have made it in New York if it

JEFFREY SWITZER

hadn't been for that. As the coach used to say, 'No pain, no gain.' "

Belushi met his wife, Judy Jacklin, now a book designer, when he was a senior and she a sophomore. "The first time I saw him was at a party," she recalls. "He was singing 'Louie, Louie' without slurring the dirty words."

Jacklin characterizes Wheaton, a Chicago suburb, as the town where "Billy Graham went to college. It is heavily Republican and totally dry—you're not even supposed to have liquor in your home. Everyone moves there so their kids can go to the right schools; so they care very much about football games and beauty contests."

After graduation in 1967, Belushi took a year to break out of the Wheaton mold. Bored by acting in summer stock and bored by a brief attempt at college, he moved to Chicago and opened the Universal Life Church Coffee House near the university with two friends, Tino Insana and Steven Beshakas. For three years they put on their own comedy production, serving the mostly student audience mu tea, Kool-Aide and passing around a jug of wine. "They were mostly tripping anyway," says Belushi. "Our subject matter was sex, drugs and violence." Dan Fogelberg was their opening act, for which they paid him seven dollars.

RAIN WORTHINGTON

Opposite: John as Elizabeth Taylor eating chicken on "Weekend Update's Celebrity Corner"; this page, left, John as Napoleon with Laraine and Steve Martin; below, as Elvis. Photo page 99: John & Dan working in their office at the studio.

EDIE BASKIN

The club was located in a tough part of Chicago, however, and the local greasers were offended by its presence. One night, one of them tried to get in without paying, and Belushi came from backstage to deal with the problem.

"I paid," said the greaser. "You calling me a liar?"

"Yeah," said Belushi, "I'm calling you a liar. Get out."

"Who are you?" said the greaser. "God?"

So Belushi pushed him out the door, threw him over a car hood and smashed him in the nose. "About fifty of his friends came out of the cracks in the sidewalk armed with boards and pipes," Belushi remembers. "There was a huge fight, but we finally got all our people inside and the show went on."

The greasers pounded on the windows during the performance and Belushi had an ever-growing bruise on his forehead as he acted. The audience didn't laugh a whole lot. Neither did the police when Belushi went to the station house with the kid whose nose he had broken.

"Who threw the first punch?" asked the sergeant.

"Ahhhhhh, I guess I did," said Belushi, grabbing the greaser's hand. "What do you say we be friends?"

That was the end of the coffeehouse, but the experience won Belushi a gig with Second City, the improvisational troupe that has served as a sort of college for comedians over the years (Dan Aykroyd, Bill Murray and Gilda Radner are also graduates of Second City). He gives director Del Close much credit for refining his technique. "Del made us explore and work with the other actors," he says. "He wanted us to take chances and not go for cheap laughs. I even took notes when he talked. It's very hard to be a good actor, you know. It's easy to be cute."

In 1973, he got a call from New York to join *National Lampoon*'s *Lemmings,* a musical production parodying the Woodstock culture, for which he perfected Joe Cocker and created the role of the announcer exhorting the chant for rain. "I chose him because he projected the feeling of a homicidal maniac," says director Tony Hendra. "Watching him act, you were always glad he hadn't taken up something more dangerous. During rehearsals, he went into a blue funk every third day and I would have to talk him out of going home to Chicago, but once he hit the stage, you knew he was in his element. He was always threatening to go over the edge, and the more dangerous the situation, the funnier."

A good example of how evenly balanced are his desires for success and destruction is how he got picked for *Saturday Night Live.* He and Aykroyd were the last hired for the cast—Aykroyd because of a reputation for not showing up at gigs, and Belushi because "I had a big chip on my shoulder. I thought all television was shit, and I let Lorne [Michaels, producer of *Saturday Night Live*] know it. My own set at home was often covered with spit. The only reason I wanted to be on it was because Michael O'Donoghue was writing and it had a chance to be good."

Belushi auditioned with his beloved samurai character (his own invention after watching a Japanese film festival on educational TV) and won a position, but his attitude was little changed. "I'd been wearing a beard for five years," he recalls. "One day Lorne suggested, 'Let's see what you look like with it off.' I came back the next day with the beard and he said, 'Why don't you just try shaving it once so we can see what it looks like?' I told him I didn't like shaving, and the next day he asked, 'Weren't you supposed to do something last night?' I told him I got sick. 'Let's see it off,' he said. So I finally shaved. My face *is* more expressive without it, I guess. And I couldn't play eleven-year-old kids in skits, like I've done, with a beard. I just grow it in the summer now."

I WANT ROBERT STIGWOOD'S legs broken!" shouts John Landis, twenty-seven-year-old director of *Animal House,* about the producer of *Sergeant Pepper.* Landis rarely talks below 110 decibels and is conceding nothing to the surrounding eaters at the Imperial Gardens, a Japanese restaurant in Los Angeles. He is the only person I have ever met who is enthusiastic about *everything.*

"That movie is the worst piece of shit I have ever seen! The worst! I wish it had been filmed on nitrate so it would disintegrate! What a piece of shit!"

John Belushi, who eats faster than any human being I have ever met, is poking at his sushi with chopsticks. If he is at all self-conscious about being stared at, or worried that Robert Stigwood has enough money to break his friend's legs, it doesn't show in his face.

Ending his tirade against Stigwood's insatiable hunger for inanity a few minutes later,

Landis points a chopstick at Belushi. "John Milius (the director of *Dillinger* and *Magnum Force* and screenwriter for Francis Ford Coppola's *Apocalypse Now)* told me that *Animal House* was the best American movie since *Patton,"* he continues to shout. "I don't know what that means, but you're his hero now. How many guys can yell 'No prisoners!' (In a final scene of *Animal House,* Bluto, Belushi's character, leads a raid on the bad guys) like John Belushi?" Landis shifts his shouting to me for a moment. "You know John did all his own stunts?"

"It's too late," says Belushi. "I told him about the rugby champion."

"Really?" shouts Landis. "That's too bad. I had everyone believing it was you."

"My own mother believes it was me swinging across the street on the sign," says Belushi. "I don't know why I had to tell him."

"Well, John did do most of his own stunts," shouts Landis. "The rugby champion double was great, though. He was very protective of John, and he would have gone out and gotten hit by cars if you'd asked him."

Steven Spielberg, director of *Jaws* and *Close Encounters of the Third Kind,* stops by the table with his girlfriend, Amy Irving *(Carrie, The Fury),* to say hello. He is, coincidentally, wearing an *Animal House* T-shirt—an omen of big bucks to come if there ever was one. "I've seen it three times," he says, sitting down at the table. "I like it because everyone gets fucked in every sense of the word. It had no cheap moralistic ending like *Barnaby Jones.* It was socially irresponsible."

"Socially irresponsible?" Landis shouts with a slight quaver. "How do you define *that?"*

Spielberg diplomatically changes the subject. "Anyway, I like the movie because it reminded me of my own college days at Cal State Long Beach. That's what I was like then. You know, Ken Kesey did one of his acid tests at a toga party we had. We filmed these pledges stealing

EDIE BASKIN

traffic lights, and all my best friends ended up in the hospital."

"We met Kesey in Oregon during the filming," says Landis.

"Yeah," adds Belushi. "I'm thinking, 'At last, I'm meeting the great Ken Kesey,' and what is the only thing he wants to hear about? Killer bees. So we did them on the show that week."

It is decided that we should all go play miniature golf. When Belushi stands, his legs and torso make a 120-degree angle, caused by a pinched nerve in his back from lifting more boxes the day before we left for the coast. Signing autographs like an overweight Groucho Marx, he makes his way slowly to the door, where we climb into Landis' station wagon. "Socially irresponsible?" Landis repeats as we drive down Sunset Boulevard. "If that were really true, he wouldn't have liked it."

"I wouldn't have been in it if it had been an immoral movie," says Belushi.

JOHN AND I ALMOST ROBBED A marina out in Ontario a couple of weeks ago," says Dan Aykroyd, Belushi's closest friend among the actors on *Saturday Night Live.* "I have some land on a lake up there, and he was helping me clear it for a cabin. When we finished, this other friend and I felt we needed a motor for our boat. As we were getting into my pickup truck—a 1941 Chrysler—John asked, 'What are you doing?' I said, 'We're going to rob the marina. Wanna come?' He said, 'Lemme get my smokes.'

"It was about two a.m. and there was a radar trap about a mile up the road, so this cop car was cruising around with its light flashing. But John was right in there with the chain cutters at the wire fence. Unfortunately, the boat trailer didn't fit the hitch on my pickup, so we didn't actually steal anything. The point here is that John is *not* into larceny. He did it for friendship. It was a matter of 'You may be crazy but you're my friend.'

"I want to stress that we did this above the border. Here, John is completely straight. In fact, he cooperates with the Justice Department and informs on drug users in the office."

JOHN BELUSHI OCCASIONALLY dismisses his audience as 'the angel-dust crowd,' but it seems as if nearly everybody loves the guy. He cannot walk down the street without being recognized every twenty feet and greeted like a long-lost crazy uncle who used to bounce you on his knee (and maybe dropped you on your head a few times).

In nearly seventy shows on *Saturday Night Live,* he has taken part in an awesome number of skits, many of which he wrote himself. He has contributed a couple of comic catch phrases to the American language—"Cheeseburger, cheeseburger" and "But nooooooo!"—just in time to replace Steve Martin's "Excuuuuuuse me!"

But no matter what role he plays, he is always John Belushi—unlike, say, Dan Aykroyd or Laraine Newman, who project little of their own personalities. Perhaps to his detriment, he is often the same violent lunatic character in whatever role he plays. Bluto in *Animal House,* for example, is not a significant departure from what he has accomplished on TV. The almost certain prospect of becoming a major star carries the danger of being typecast as a maniac for the rest of his life and ultimately boring his fans.

I doubt this will happen, because he would bore himself first. He could have spent the rest of his life as a killer bee, but he stopped before it became stale. He also has too many other talents. He and Aykroyd formed the Blues Brothers to warm up audiences before the show, ultimately made an appearance and now have a contract with Atlantic Records. They will open for Steve Martin at the Universal Amphitheatre in Los Angeles in September. The album will be live (the backup band is as yet unchosen) and the cover will probably feature them changing a flat on the Blues-mobile.

Belushi's plans are hard to pin down. Depending on his mood, he will be happy doing *Saturday Night Live* for the rest of his life or never again (he has one year left on his contract). And he might do another movie, depending on if he can stand all the assholes in Hollywood.

His wife, Judy, who ought to know when to take him at his word, says he wants to be a serious actor. "In college I saw him play Danforth in *The Crucible,* and he was so intense that the other actors thought he was going to hurt them," she says. "When he does get a straight role he will blow people away."

IN GLEN GLENN SOUND STUDIOS

in Los Angeles, they are about to loop (that is, overdub) *Old Boyfriends* so they can sell it to television.

"We have to get rid of all the fucks and cunts and piles of crap," says director Joan Twekesbury kissing John Belushi hello. "This is for the TV version."

"Pile of crap?" says Belushi. "You can say that on TV."

"You sure?"

"Listen, I've been fighting the censors for three years. I ought to know."

"Well, okay," concedes Tewkesbury. "But be thinking about substitutes for the other words."

The movie (due for fall release) stars Talia Shire, Rocky's girlfriend, as a woman who looks up her old boyfriends in order to avenge past humiliations. Belushi plays a guy who took her out in high school, ripped off her panties, wrapped them around a basketball and dribbled them down the court at a pep rally. She meets him again at age thirty-three in St. Paul, where he is singing lead in a rock band at high-school proms and renting tuxedos to students. In the scene Tewkesbury is looping, Shire drives Belushi to lovers' lane and becomes very aggressive. He doesn't know what to make of it at all.

"You college girls are all alike," he says in the movie. "You talk, talk, talk, when what you want is to fuck, fuck, fuck,"

"How about neck, neck, neck?" suggests Tewkesbury.

'I'm not going to say *that!*" objects Belushi at the microphone.

"Bang, bang, bang? asks Tewkesbury.

"How about, '... when what you want is sex, sex, sex'?"

Tewkesbury agrees, and they play the sentence about ten times before Belushi is synched exactly with the proper tone of voice. They play the rest of the scene—Shire takes off Belushi's pants, bids him to get out of the car so she can "rape" him on the ground, then drives off to leave him clad in his boxer shorts.

The character is apparently quite worried about his potence while Shire is unzipping his pants. "It didn't work out so well the last time I was up here," he says.

I laugh, and Belushi points at me. "What are you writing in your notebook? You fucker!"

"I'm writing you can't get it up."

"I'll kill you when we get out of here," he yells. "I'll kill you!"

Any other actor would be proud of such an effective scene. But not John Belushi, the former middle linebacker who loses his mind every Saturday night in front of millions of people for laughs. The Belushi up there on the screen is vulnerable in a way I've never seen before, achingly so. Maybe it's more fun to be a macho maniac, but this is great acting.

"It's not me, it's the role," moans Belushi. "I have to keep telling myself it's not me...."

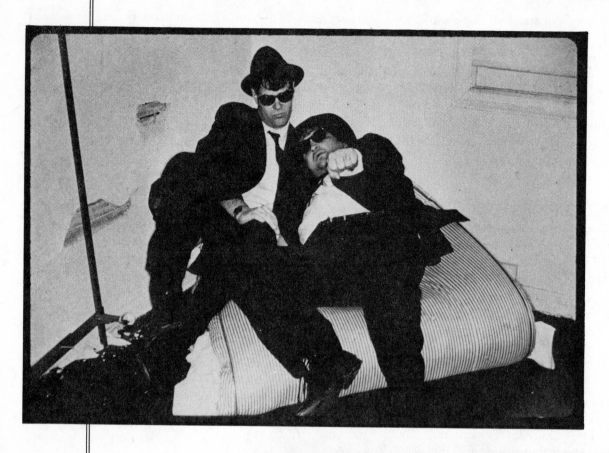

PHOTOGRAPHS BY ANNIE LEIBOVITZ

BLUES
Brothers

BY
TIMOTHY
WHITE

HERE'S THE STRAIGHT POOP: every hapless hambone stranded in this sorry life should *at least* have a main squeeze who knows how to clean his clocks, an unholy soul band that this twosome can do the *Do* to, and a copacetic little gin mill where they can work this blissful bit of juju.

Now that's a sweet little vi-sion, but it's *not* the Big Picture. The Big Picture, unfortunately, is that there is a wealth of chowderheads, mean-spirited stiffs and marginally adjusted jerks out there upon whom such a blessing would be squandered. I'm not trying to sit in anybody's lunch, so to speak, but some people in this world wouldn't know a good time if they chipped a tooth on it. I feel at this moment that most of the people who reside in the totemlike townhouses of Manhattan's moneyed Turtle Bay area should never be privy to a piece of heaven like Jake and Elwood's legendary Big Apple hideaway, the Blues Bar.

You see, Turtle Bay is a cool, crusty enclave in the east 40s where every Saturday night soiree seems more like one of those reptilian Tuesday cocktail quip-a-thons where the icy hors d'oeuvres never get touched, where the tart white wine goes down like Janitor in a Drum, and where every chattering mannequin is auditioning for a fat cat's lap. "What a marvelous collection of contemptible crumbs," I'm thinking to myself when my goodnatured chum, Miami, pulls me over into a corner and rules that it's definitely time to slip out of this mortuary and go where folks know how to get on the good foot.

"So wherezat?" I slur.

"The Blues Bar," he whispers desperately.

"Huh?"

"You know, Jake 'n Elwood's hangout."

Jake and El—oh, you mean the Blues Brothers!" I say, brightening considerably at the memory of their unbridled treatment of "Soul Man" on *Saturday Night Live* earlier this evening. "They hang out at some place in the city? You mean there really is a Black Rhino Club?"

"Nah," he hisses, *"the Rhino thing is just a routine on the show. But Jake and Elwood get loose at the Blues Bar on certain nights—and tonight's one of 'em!"*

"Where is this place?"

"You'll see."

THE RIDE TO OUR ARCANE DEStination is a long, bleary bumpalong through some pretty nasty neighborhoods. At length, we pull up to this forlorn little saloon with pitch-black windows.

"There's nobody around here. This place has been shut down for years," I protest as Miami pushes me out of the taxi.

"That's what you think, joyboy," he chuckles as he taps on the side door and barks, "Big Jake summoned us!"

When the door swings wide, I sober up in a hurry. Looming in the doorway is a big drink of water in a taut T-shirt and shades, the guy

flexing biceps the size of my waist. It's Matt "Guitar" Murphy, one-time member of James Cotton's band and now thundering alongside Steve "The Colonel" Cropper in the Blues Brothers' band.

"Come on in, Miami," Murphy laughs, "and bring your funny-looking pal. The beer's ice cold and we got a lotta nice *snug-geets* in here t'night."

"Snug-geets?"

"That's what Matt calls his women," my friend explains as we wade into an ecstatic dancing crowd that fills every inch of the small, cozy room. A jukebox stocked with every jump blues and R&B single of any lasting significance is blaring a Sam and Dave tune and the walls are plastered with faded snapshots of the Blues Brothers posed in front of most of the gas stations, roadhouses and jails between New York and Calumet City, Illinois. In the majority of the photos, the sunglassed group is either holding someone, or being held, at gunpoint.

"Who *took* these shots?"

Miami looks at me like I'm a dunce. "Fans—who else?"

"And who's asking!?" roars a voice.

Shaken, I turn to face the Black Rhino himself, Joliet Jake Blues. Built big, badassed and close to the ground, Jake is decked out in his customary baggy black serge suit, sweat-stained white shirt and ribbon-thin black tie. Rising behind him is broad-shouldered Elwood, his younger brother, sidekick and silent confidant, who's a mite less formally attired in these wee hours, having stripped down to a sleeveless T-shirt and black vest. But both men are wearing midnight fedoras and shades that, even in the red light, accent their sinister barroom pallors.

"Is this clown a friend of yours?" an unsmiling Jake snaps at Miami, who nods cautiously, introducing me. "Well, I hope he came here to listen to the blues, get shitfaced drunk and fall

down on the floor," Jake rules as Elwood shifts his stance threateningly.

I nod very cautiously.

"Well then," Joliet laughs, giving me a mighty bear hug, "lemme fill the biggest mug I can find for ya!"

Stunned, I stand amidst the melee as my hefty host hunkers over to the bar and tells Keith Richards, one of the guest bartenders (along with Richard Dreyfuss and Atlantic Records Senior Vice President Michael Klenfner) to fetch a tall draft. But the biggest jolt comes when silent Elwood steps forward, extends his hand and *speaks,* asking me if I enjoyed *Briefcase Full of Blues.* "S-s-sounded pretty decent to me," I sputter, and as we shake on it I notice a heavy gold chain trailing from his handcuffed wrist to a black leather briefcase.

Suddenly, Jake is back with my beer and suggesting very strongly that I drink it in one gulp. As my eyes water from the effort both men vanish in a puff of truly rank cigar smoke.

JAKE AND ELWOOD ARE TWO mysterious pieces of work," the huge, mustachioed Klenfner later concurs. "Either one is capable of appearing or disappearing at any damned moment, but silent Elwood's the queerest case—he's gone in a flash and nobody knows where the hell he went. Elwood's never too comfortable, especially around groups of people, but then he could be rolling around naked in a tub of whipped cream and still not feel comfortable. So he just splits. It drives me so crazy I've thought about getting one of those Batman-type spotlights to shine in the air at night whenever we need to contact him. Instead of a bat symbol silhouetted against the sky, we'd either project a giant pair of sunglasses—Ray-Bans No. 5022-G15—or his silhouette. I don't know, it's a problem I haven't solved yet."

Well, it must be the only one. Klenfner's new act has produced a runaway hit single ("Soul Man") and a platinum album that contains some of the most exhilarating music of an especially bleak winter. The Blues Brothers and their record have been dubbed a "novelty" in this disco-dominated era, and, considering its long heritage of work with blues and R&B artists, Klenfner is especially pleased their aggressive R&B sound triumphed on the Atlantic label.

"I think their second album is gonna do even better," he enthuses. "We've got the best band working anywhere, and on the road Jake and Elwood prove they have the chops to–"

"But Michael," I interrupt. "There's one thing that bothers me about the Blues Brothers. I can't shake the screwy feeling that I've seen 'em some place before. I mean, exactly *who* are they? Jake, for example, looks a fuck of a lot like John Belu–"

"Now *listen,*" Klenfner says gruffly. "I don't know any more about them than you do. All I know is they sound great and act awful goddamned strange.

"I'll tell you this: they're gonna be on the bill on the New Year's Eve show at the closing of Winterland out in San Francisco. Why don't you fly out? I can promise you a great show and

a great time, but as for getting the Blues Brothers' inside story, you're on your own. Far as I'm concerned, what you *hear* is what they *are.*"

WHAT A GOD-DAMNED GOOD

band!" Bill Graham yells to Klenfner over the din of an afternoon soundcheck rendition of "Jailhouse Rock." Holding on to his own crumpled, gray version of a Blues Brothers hat, he darts around the vacant, drafty floor of Winterland issuing orders.

"So what the hell did you expect?" Klenfner bellows back as Jake and Elwood put the group through their paces. "Naturally we got the best!" At this point the band members are a well-rehearsed bundle of nerves. Few major reviews have yet appeared on *Briefcase* and the Brothers & Co. feel like interlopers on a bill that places their act between a short set by the New Riders of the Purple Sage and an all-night epic concert by the Grateful Dead. Camped on the sidewalk outside are hard-core Deadheads, and the only indications that this anxious hippie throng might have any familiarity with the Blues Brothers are a couple of dazed backpackers wearing battered plastic coneheads.

"Three hours till we open!" Graham shouts as the horns persevere. Led by Tom "Bones" Malone on sax, trombone and trumpet, the distinguished lineup (Lou "Blue Lou" Marini, tenor sax; Alan "Mr. Fabulous" Rubin, trumpet; Tom "Triple Scale" Scott, tenor sax) is skintight by the second take when they're joined by Steve Cropper, Matt Murphy, keyboardman Paul Shaffer and the funky ballistics of bassist Donald "Duck" Dunn and drummer Steve "Getdwa" Jordan. Jake decides to grab the mike and leans way back for a growling assault on the "Jailhouse" chorus while Elwood punctuates the proceedings with some honkin' blues harp.

But in a finger snap it's a wrap, and the band

mills around the hall as mammoth breakaway plastic bags full of balloons are hoisted to the ceiling in preparation for the New Year countdown. Meanwhile, Jake and Elwood have now dematerialized. It takes the rest of the afternoon to locate the dingy hotel room they're holed up in, but my reconnaissance pays off. Their reticence virtually dissolved by a late breakfast of tepid Muskatel and some overripe seafood, both open up for the first in-depth interview of their convoluted career.

"Elwood!" Jake howls, drawing his partner's catatonic attention from the high-school football game flickering on the TV. "How do you think the Blues Brothers are gonna do tonight? Do we have a chance against the Dead and all the Deadheads?"

Elwood hesitates before speaking, flashing me a wounded glance.

"Jake, I gotta say no way, man. They're gonna blow us off the stage."

"It's a nightmare," Jake agrees. "They'll be screaming, 'Grateful Dead! We want Garcia!' "

" 'Get offstage, you swine!' Elwood joins in. " 'Get fucking *lost!*' "

"Oh no they won't!" scolds a shadowy female figure in the next room. She is laying out their black suits and slipping extra pairs of sunglasses in their breast pockets; Foster Grants for Jake, Ray-Bans (No. 5022-G15) for Elwood. I realize it's Jake's spectral spouse, known only as the Blues Wife. "You guys are wrong!" she begs. "They'll be screaming Colonel, Bones, Joliet, *El-wood!*"

"I'm not so sure," Elwood sighs. "Right about now I'd like a bottle of Night Train wine—with a little spike of Sterno in it—to cheer me up. But hell, that swill is up to a buck-seventy a fifth!"

"Key Largo was another great brand," Jake chimes in wistfully. " 'Just one sip/And you will *know*/That you're on the island/Of Key Largo.' So what do *you* wanna know?" he asks, pointing a menacing finger at me.

"To begin with, the word is Universal is planning a Blue Brothers film, and Elwood is writing the script."

"The Scriptatron XL 9000 has to finish the script," Elwood recites mechanically. "It'll be the first screenplay by the amazing Scriptatron XL 9000; the first fully programmed script. It's almost half finished."

"But what's the plot? Some say it's the story of your veiled past."

"Yeah," Jake admits, scratching the bristly soul patch under his lower lip with a shrimp tail. "We play ourselves. Here's a simple synopsis: it starts with me getting out of jail after three years and I expect the band to still be together. . . ."

"He got three years on a five-year rap," Elwood interrupts. "Armed robbery at a gas station. I was driving but he took the rap because he knew I would string myself up if I went to jail. He did it for the *band.*"

"Well, the band demanded their per diem," Jake explains, "so I had to rob the place! But anyhow, the film is about finding the band members and trying to get it all back together again."

"We hunt them down like cops, like *detectives,*" Elwood bubbles. "We have nothing, a scrap of paper with their last phone numbers and a coupla old addresses. We discover that each one now has a different trip; a couple of 'em are living suburban lives, mostly working day jobs. We were just getting hot when Jake went in the slammer, drawing big crowds in highway drinking halls. Now we've re-formed to try again!"

"It's like *The Magnificent Seven,*" yells Jake, "or *Force Ten from Navarrone!*"

The liner notes on the back of their album jacket inferred that they grew up in orphanages, took a lot of grief from frustrated nuns, learned the blues from a black janitor named Curtis and staked out Calumet City, Illinois, as their stompin' grounds . . .

"Right," Elwood confirms, "but that wasn't the half of it.

"Both of us were victims of heavy corporal punishment as children," he reveals somberly. "And there's a scene in the movie, in fact, where we go back to one of the orphanages to fulfill a promise we made to a nun. We're both sitting in these little school desks, and Big Jake's wedged in, he's stuck, and she whacks the shit out of us with a steel-edge ruler. She's like a kendo artist. She moves in on us, and then vanishes because Jake says the 'F' word in front of her! The school is named St. Helen of the Blessed Shroud Orphanage and the nun's name is Sister Mary Stigmata.

"There are blood references everywhere in the film and the halls of this orphanage are filled with the images of martyred priests, these grotesque statues of clergymen strung up years ago by pagans. It's a school for special children now but the subsidies have all fallen out from under it, the church won't support it anymore, and Sister Stigmata is really strapped for bucks. They're gonna ship her off to a mission if she can't keep up the rent.

"Now, she's the only family we have, see?" Elwood says passionately, "but she threw us out and said, 'Don't come back until you redeem yourselves! You're thieves and liars, so clear out!' It's a big Catholic guilt trip she lays on us, but we *are* thieves and [*big grin*] filthy-mouthed liars! So we come back and decide to do her a favor and raise some money for the school.

"We're pretty strapped financially at this point. I've got a job but I put most of the money into our car, the Blues Mobile, which is an ex-Indiana state police car with a 440 in it—from the preunleaded gas era. The speedometer just says 'certified calibration' and it's clocked for 140. All through the movie you'll see close-ups of the speedometer, the needle just banging in there at 130.

"We bought it at a municipal auction. We used to have a Cadillac, which I traded for a microphone, and Jake goes nuts when he sees this old Dodge I'm driving around in, but I soon prove to Jake how fast the Dodge is.

"And it helps during an incredible car chase at the end of the movie," he says with a sly wink.

"By the way, how did you assemble the original band?"

"It was agony," says Jake, burying his fat face in his hands. "Elwood and I were a duo and when word got out we were forming a group, I got phone calls immediately, calls from heavy stars, saying, 'I wanna be in your band!' And it was a question of whether to assemble one or just get a band that was already established—some guys together for ten years so we could put 'em up there and let 'em just groove. I was thinking about getting Delbert McClinton's band, and Roomful of Blues, too. When we first resurfaced, Elwood and I did a gig at the Lone Star Cafe in New York in June [of 1978] with Roomful of Blues.

"But finally we just decided, 'Fuck the cost and the damage it will do to the feelings of people who aren't asked, and let's go for the best band we can get, *piece by piece.*' We got Bones Malone first and he recommended Cropper and Dunn. We really didn't know who they were," Jake snorts. "Then when he [Malone] said, 'You know, from "Knock on Wood" and "Soul Man," ' we said, 'Would *they* do it?!'

"I called them up, acting real arrogant," Jake recounts, "saying, '*Welllll,* all right Cropper, you're in the group but you're a rhythm guitar player—ya got that?' and he went [*meekly*], 'I *like* playing rhythm guitar; I don't like all that lead stuff.' So I said [*sarcastically*], 'Oh, you're hard to work with, aren't ya?'

"Then I called Dunn up and said, 'I never met you but I'd like you to be in a group—but I understand you don't get along with Cropper.' He said, '*Aw no, we get along all right!*' I was just giving them all kinda shit, bustin' their balls," Jake guffaws, slapping Elwood on the back.

"But they both said yes, and, uh, incidentally . . . they didn't know who *we* were either."

"Wasn't your first public reappearance on a 1975 segment of *Saturday Night Live* in which you dressed in bee costumes and played 'King Bee'?"

Their heads bob . . . warily.

"At that time, I'd do anything to sing," counsels Jake contritely. "So they got us into these stupid bee costumes. Boy, that was a dog performance."

"I'm intrigued by this longstanding affiliation with *Saturday Night Live*," I press them. "How close are your ties to the show? You know, the more I look at Elwood, the more he reminds me of Dan Aykr—"

"Well, gotta split now," they yelp in unison. "Er, hope you like the show tonight!"

I DO, AND I'M NOT ALONE. A shoulder-to-shoulder army of Deadheads rushes the stage when Jake and Elwood scramble on to a tumultuous fanfare of "I Can't Turn You Loose," Jake turning cartwheels as they erupt next with "Hey Bartender." The program is identical to the album, but it takes on a uniquely exultant tone as the group becomes aware that the audience knows every number.

Indeed, halfway through the set, Jake looks up to spy several willowy longhairs decked out in basic black getups identical to his own. A deafening salvo greets the familiar twanging lead-guitar intro to "Soul Man" and the victory

is complete by the time the Brothers close with " 'B' Movie Box Car Blues."

The group overruns the stage when they do their encore, and Jake's cartwheel choreography is out of hand when "Flip, Flop & Fly" segues into the unhinged "Jailhouse Rock."

Backstage afterward, the dressing room floods with well-wishers, and even a cantankerous old grizzly like Jake is so moved by the adulation that he removes his Foster Grants and presents them to a deeply touched young fan—although Joliet quickly replaces them with a spare pair he had stashed in his breast pocket.

The Jefferson Starship turns over its Airplane-era Victorian house on Fulton Street for a post-concert Blues Brothers party, but as the evening wears on, there are rumors among the 300-odd guests that Jake and Elwood won't show. Spirits are momentarily lifted when *Saturday Night Live* stalwarts Laraine Newman and Bill Murray stroll and stumble, respectively, in . . . followed shortly afterward by John Belushi and Dan Aykroyd, but disappointment blankets the crowd as it becomes apparent that 1979's conquering heroes will be a no-show.

Some critics have noted that the Blues Brothers' musical direction and their decision to record their debut LP live at the Universal Ampitheatre in L.A. bespeak a vitality and an unabashed sense of fun that is currently in short supply. Although their show consists entirely of a roundup of R&B and blues oldies, each was picked and refurbished with genuine enthusiasm. And sometimes their feelings for the music run still deeper. Stax/Volt veterans Steve Cropper and Duck Dunn say that it was a special thrill to resurrect some of their vintage material; the night before the band left for their nine-night stand in Los Angeles, Cropper listened to some Otis Redding records for the first time since Redding's death, Steve's eyes welling up with emotion at the sound of his old boss' searing vocals.

As a band, the Blues Brothers are a delight. As a musical force they are merely a friendly reminder of some great music that in recent years has largely been ignored or forgotten. There's more to popular music than the "pre-programmed electronic disco" Elwood disdains, and the Blues Brothers remind us of this fact with humor and spirit.

I wander upstairs for what proves to be a fascinating conversation with Dan Aykroyd, but feel a little badly because Joliet Jake had vowed earlier that we would have a last chat. I've come to realize that the positive energy emanating from the Blues Brothers is something of an elixir in these jaded times, and I'm pissed off I won't be getting another hit of it.

Wrung out and kinda bummed, I decided to drown my already sodden sorrows sometime around 4:30 a.m. by swigging from various bottles of champagne being passed around the mansion, and soon discover my depression is being cemented by an unexpected dose of acid. Cursing myself for forgetting what Bill Graham had advised earlier ("Don't eat or drink anything being passed around tonight if you don't want to trip"), I race around the house in mounting terror. Luckily, I collide with Cynthia Bowman, the pretty national publicity director for the Starship, who commandeers Michael Klenfner's waiting limousine and sternly instructs the bewildered chauffeur to take me back to the nearby Miyako Hotel, posthaste.

Grateful for the assistance, I lean out the window to thank her as the car pulls away from the curb and look up to see that her face has become a hideous kaleidoscope. I'm jolted speechless; I've never done acid before and the sight scares me out of my wits.

After a seemingly endless excursion through predawn San Franciso—during which I momentarily became convinced that the driver is a horned demon taking me, willy-nilly, down into the Stygian depths of hell—I find myself sitting outside the comforting Oriental familiarity of the Miyako. Somehow I make it to the suite that I'm sharing with Miami.

"Fuck me dead!" I rage as he opens the door. "I got dosed by some low-life scuzz at the Blues Brothers party and now I'm tripping straight out of my skull."

Miami's jaw drops and he leads me in gingerly, telling me to lay down and try to remain calm while he makes a phone call. I am too distracted by the colorful streams of insects surging up the room's melting walls to get a fix on his telephone conversation, but minutes later the door swings wide and in strides a formidable slice of reality, John Belushi and his wife, Judy Jacklin.

To make a long story short, the Belushis, with whom I have only an acquaintance, stay with me for hours, John assuming a comforting bedside manner as we shoot the shit until I am exhausted enough to doze off with the help of Valium; his kindness reminding me of one additional thing every hapless hambone should have in this life: a couple of unexpected friends.

I never do see the Black Rhino again that weekend but I remember Belushi smiling at the tail end of my trip when I mentioned Joliet Jake's latest disappearance. "Aw, don't worry about it; I think you should have these," he said soothingly, placing something dark and gleaming upon the night table as I drifted into sleep.

When I wake up late that afternoon my head is full of questions. Squinting about, trying to get my bearings, the first thing I see is the San Francisco skyline reflected in a shiny object lying just across from my head.

I blink and realize that it's the gift I was given the night before . . . Jake's spare pair of Foster Grants.

EDIE BASKIN

DAN Aykroyd

BY TIMOTHY WHITE

My parents have a photo of Dan when he was about three and I was just a small protein unit, and in the picture he's riding a small motorcycle, carrying a machine gun, and wearing a cowboy hat. In other words, even then he had at least three characters going at once.

— PETER AYKROYD
Dan's funny younger brother

EASTER SATURDAY 1978, 7:30 p.m.: *"Now what in the hell am I supposed to do with these claws?!"*

Portly, pissed off John Belushi stomps down a gloomy hallway at NBC's *Saturday Night Live* studio in New York after rehearsing a skit due to air this evening called "The Thing That Wouldn't Leave." Dressed in washed out jeans and a baggy sweatshirt, with large floppy green claws covering his hands and feet, Belushi is as disgusted as the suburban couple (Jane Curtin, Bill Murray) he torments in the skit. Grunting a hello, he lumbers into his dressing room, plops down and bites a banana.

Then he simultaneously swallows the fruit and spits out the peel.

"I'm not gonna wear these stupid claws, they're too weird, make no sense," he pouts, pulling them from his hands and throwing them against the door as Dan Aykroyd steps into the room. Dan is wearing a collarless, candy-striped shirt with elbow garters, red apron and straw hat. Tonight he will do one of his bizarrely credible pitchman segments, in this case hawking a new fast-food treat: barbecued bunnies.

"Hello there, Thing," he calls out affectionately. The appearance of Aykroyd is a welcome relief; with his bright, twinkling eyes, boyish face and courtly manner he's obviously the saner of the two. As Belushi begins to bitch with great resonance about the raw deal—"bullshit money, no points, but I'm gonna be a fucking star anyhow, those cheap bastards"—he got for starring in some forthcoming film comedy called *National Lampoon's Animal House,* Danny and I have a pleasant chat about each other's plans for the holiday weekend.

I move further away from Belushi as he begins spitting pieces of banana peel at the *Animal House* poster taped to his mirror—*Sploff!* "Ha! Those motherfuckers!" I am about to broaden the range of my discourse with Aykroyd, who's been leafing idly through a magazine, when he suddenly comes upon an article on the penile transducer, a *Clockwork Orange*-inspired bit of hardware used in the treatment of sex criminals.

"Aversion therapy!" Aykroyd shouts with sufficient glee to knock his own hat off, then delves into the text with salacious enthrallment. I glance from one man to the other, increasingly unnerved as Aykroyd whoops at each psychosexual revelation and John twitches his claw feet and vents his anger with mounting velocity. I steal away, convinced that both actors are off the beam, but finally deciding that from the claws up, Belushi is, pound for pound, the more *alien* of the two.

Until I later learn about Aykroyd's feet.

It seems that the man has more in common with the Thing than meets the eye, by which I

This page, "The Untouchables," with Dan as Elliot Ness; opposite, as Leonard Pinth-Garnell, host of "Bad Playhouse."

EDIE BASKIN

EDIE BASKIN

Think about it. For more than 120 Saturday nights he's come into our homes and made acting on live television look *easy*. A comedic Lon Chaney, this Funny Man of a Thousand Faces has mimicked with unerring accuracy some of the greatest figures of our time. His Jimmy Carter sendup captures the president's ineptitude-masking fascination for folksy banality and quasi-hipness with an unctuous schoolboy drawl and a Cheshire cat grin. Still more devastating are his impersonations of Richard Nixon, each nervous facet of this broken-down Cro-Magnon crook sharpened to a cutting edge, from Dick's apelike shoulder roll and phlebitic shuffle, to his chomping, jowl-quivering monotone and his mail-chute smile.

"I look at him as a bird of prey, with that hawk-lipped way about him," Dan asserts. "Tremendous magnetism. God, he's charismatic."

"Most comedians or actors will try characters out on you from time to time to see if they work," explains Michael O'Donoghue, a former *Saturday Night Live* writer/performer. "But with Danny, they just seem to leap out of nowhere. It's utterly startling because you think he can do anything; he can just make it up, fully realized, on the spot."

mean that, well, I don't know how to break this to you all, but there happens to be this thin membrane of skin tissue that connects his toes, specifically the second and third toes. Of each foot. As Danny phrases it, he's a "genetic mutant," but that sounds a trifle indelicate. Let's just say that Dan Aykroyd, the handsome, talented star of TV's *Saturday Night Live,* the hero of millions and an inspiration to youth . . . has webbed feet.

JOHN BELUSHI IS EVERYMAN'S superstar; Gilda Radner is America's sweetheart; Bill Murray is the oddball celebrity's celebrity, but Dan Aykroyd is a precise *blur,* moving slow enough to be seen clearly, but much too fast to be categorized.

Aykroyd's night gallery of alter egos is voluminous, including such difficult subjects as Elliot Ness, Orson Welles/Citizen Kane, Julia Child, Clark Gable, both Scotty and Bones from *Star Trek,* plus such regional and/or dialect characters as curt southern state troopers, randy midwestern rubes, proud Aberdeen Scotch guards, mincing French waiters, and snobbish British theater critics—not to mention creations like Beldar Conehead, sleazy cable-TV personality E. Buzz Miller, and his Jorge Festrunk to Steve Martin's brother Yortuk in the "Czech Brothers" routines.

"I had no idea the 'Czech Brothers' would be as popular as they are," says Aykroyd. "Steve had a character called the 'Continental Suave Guy'; I saw him do him in his act one night and I really enjoyed it. I went backstage afterward and I said, 'Listen, I do this Czech architect.'. . . I'd noticed a tremendous similarity in the rhythms of Steve's character and I said, 'Let's put them both together as Czechs who wear polyester shirts and everything!' It didn't work that well with the studio audience the first time we did it on the show, but then we got so much feedback from people who watched it on TV. Phew! Really blew me away."

Just as popular as the "wild and crazy guys" are the Coneheads. "The Coneheads were originally a drawing of mine," says Aykroyd with a low chuckle. "I was watching these heads on TV one night and I thought, 'Fuck, wouldn't it be neat if they were four or five inches *higher?*' I put the whole Remulak thing together with one of the writers, Tom Davis.

"We were gonna call them pinheads," he adds soberly, "but we decided no 'cause we didn't want to offend anybody who had encephalitis."

When Aykroyd wishes to offend, he does so masterfully, as with his huckster spiels for useless appliances like the Moth-Masher or the electric blender that liquefies uncleaned fish called the Super Bass-O-Matic. It's no accident that he's adept at duplicating the machine-gun, doggerel prose of TV-commercial pitchmen, having worked as one for a cable-TV station in Toronto, CITY-TV's Channel 79.

Aykroyd's most off-putting guise is that of Irwin Mainway, a crass, oily entrepreneur with a pencil mustache who possesses all the moral fiber of a doorknob. "He's the ultimate urban businessman—the true hawker," says Aykroyd in admiration. "Have you ever been to one of those joints where they auction appliances off the street? The guy has a mike around his neck and he talks a five-dollar clock radio up to thirty-three bucks! This is how Mainway star-

ted. He was one of those barkers and most of his goods were hot. Now he's evolved into a business executive and he goes on talk shows for publicity and to push and defend his really bad, harmful products: fur coats made from near extinct animals, a kid's toy called Bag o' Glass. . . ."

Mainway recently turned up on the consumer awareness program, *On the Spot,* hosted by the aggressive Jane Face (Jane Curtin). The discussion concerned the unusual menu for his school-lunch catering service.

FACE: "Mr. Mainway, isn't it true that on last April 18th, the school children of this city ate a hot lunch composed almost entirely of puréed insects?!"
MAINWAY: "Hey, come on, gimme a break. I gotta find out what dese kids like!"

The same canny respect that informs Aykroyd's Irwin Mainway illuminates his stunning Tom Snyder. The rumpled tan leisure suit is there, and the volcanic horse laughs, aimlessly waving arms, and smug, pseudo-absorbed slouch. But Aykroyd also captures the desperation of Snyder's pursed-lip cigarette puffing, and the empty-headed "by gosh" and references to "the boys" that the perpetually ill-prepared *Tomorrow* host employs to buy time.

Snyder himself is so rattled by the way Aykroyd nails him that he once attempted to confront the caricature by inviting an NBC page on his show to try to top Danny; and when that fizzled, Tom leapt in and sought to imitate *Aykroyd* imitating *him* with a bumbling compulsiveness that was as pathetic as it was spellbinding.

Aykroyd's ability to mirror and then expand on any character he chooses—prominent or not—borders on the soul-snatching power of obeah. Thanks to Dan Aykroyd, we know things about Nixon, Carter and Snyder that they themselves could not have shown us. And poor Tom; if he wanted to retaliate (i.e., save face), what he should have done was attempt to mimic *Dan Aykroyd*. But the Funny Man of a Thousand Faces is also the Man in the Shadows. Quite simply, none of us knows who the devil Dan Aykroyd is.

BORN IN OTTAWA, CANADA, AND raised in Hull, Quebec ("where Montreal sends its old gangsters to cool out"), twenty-six-year-old Daniel Edward Aykroyd is the son of Samuel Cuthbert Peter Hugh Aykroyd, a Canadian government official of English-Anglican descent whose lineage traces back to a fourteenth-century constable of Wadsworth, England, and the former Lorraine Gougeon, the Norman-French daughter of a farmer who also served as a Royal Canadian Mounted Policeman.

Described by younger son Peter Jonathan, 23, as a "seasoned bureaucrat," the senior Mr. Aykroyd rose from a middle-echelon post in the policy-making Privy Council to assistant deputy minister of transport for research and development. Careerwise, Danny headed in the opposite direction from his strait-laced father, cutting a footloose swath through various fine schools in Quebec and Ontario, among them the St. Pius X Minor Preparatory Seminary for boys and Carleton University in Ottawa. Both Aykroyd boys maintained an abiding interest in comic acting, and Peter followed Danny into Toronto's improvisational theater company, Second City. Danny's big pre-*Saturday Night Live* break was the role of a "Jackie Gleason antagonist-type" janitor in a Canadian Broadcasting Company TV comedy for children called *Coming Up Rosie*.

Upon meeting Dan Aykroyd, one is impressed with his gentleness, his deference and, where his various hobbies (motorcycles, architecture, armaments, aeronautics, almost anything involving intricate machinery) and profession are concerned, an overwhelming intensity.

This intensity is best illustrated by the on-location proceedings during Aykroyd's first day of shooting with *Coming Up Rosie*. Aykroyd arose on the morning of Friday the thirteenth and dutifully reported to the *Rosie* offices at CBC-TV, despite a killer flu and a temperature of 104. The first scene called for foreign secret agents to scurry through a car wash, and Danny, wearing a black hat, did so without hesitation. When he emerged from the other end—coughing, sneezing and sopping wet—much of the hat's indelible dye had been transferred to his face.

Undaunted, the black-faced Aykroyd completed the morning's shooting without complaint and then came back for more in the afternoon, the day's chores culminating in a key rooftop chase scene in which the tireless foreigners run an adversary around a skylight.

Overzealous to the last, Aykroyd decided to ad-lib a spectacular five-foot leap over the skylight. Regrettably, he sailed short of the mark and plunged through the wired glass to a warehouse floor some twenty-five feet below, hitting two light standards on the way down and landing on his ass.

The cast and crew were horror struck, with much shrieking and hysterics all around. Rushing to the shattered skylight, the cameramen peered in to see an unhurt, twenty-two-year-old Dan Aykroyd screaming back up to them, *"Hey, you guys! Did you get the shot?!"*

AFTER FLYING INTO SAN FRANcisco for the Blues Brothers show at Winterland on New Year's Eve, I was fortunate to learn that Belushi and Aykroyd were also in town for the event, the two taking a break from the L.A. filming of director Steven Spielberg's work-in-progress, *1941* (in which they play a pilot and a tank commander, respectively). I take a room—along with my cohort Miami—at the Miyako Hotel where John and Danny are staying and arrange to interview Aykroyd for a separate profile. He gives his tentative consent and then . . . nothing. He successfully evades me thereafter—until I persuade Belushi to intervene on my behalf.

"He's a little hard to pin down," explains John as we sit together in his suite, "and he's very suspicious of the press, but you'll have no problems now."

Sure enough, there's a brisk knock at the door and in hastens Dan Aykroyd, dripping wet and clad only in an orange bath towel. Nonetheless, his mind is now clearly made up. He pops a beer and props his webbed feet on a room service cart, calling happily for the first question.

"Say, I hear you've been playing a mean harmonica since your early teens," I begin.

"Since I was sixteen," he nods with zest. "I jammed with Muddy Waters once, too—but that was on drums. He was fuckin' great! It was at a club called Le Hibou, which means 'the owl.'

"Incidentally, John is the Owl too," he informs with affection, "and he's also the Bear Man, and the Black Hole in Space, and the Thing, and I also like to refer to him secretly as . . . *the Black Rhino.*"

Belushi, presently engaged in a heated phone conversation, cups the receiver and roars with considerable annoyance, "Did he say I was the Black Rhino? *Don't you listen to him!*"

"I have a company now called Black Rhino Enterprises," Aykroyd beams, suddenly speaking in a clipped, businesslike fashion. "Part of it is a T-shirt marketing thing. . . . Where the Black Rhino comes from," he confides, "is that I had a dream one night that I was living way up on this cliff in Canada, overlooking this snow-strewn waste. There was this snorting rhino chained in the backyard. And I looked at it and the face started to look a lot like Belushi," he giggles. "And he was snorting hard and ripping up the backyard and I went out and tossed meat to him. I placated him,

helped him, and I realized [*his eyes glaze over goofily*], '*I need this force in my life.*'"

"But doesn't someone else share the same nickname?" I ask. "As I recall Jake Bl–"

"Belushi is *also* the Black Hole in Space," he overrules, "because, you'll notice, if you ever lend him a watch or a lighter or something, it goes through him into another dimension. You ask for it back five minutes later and it's gone and there's no way you can find it. Really.

"He's like a hurricane!" Danny proclaims with a ringmaster's flourish. "He's the Black Hole in Space!"

Belushi, still on the phone, makes an ugly face that dissolves into a big, sloppy grin.

Watching the two friends go at each other, their Frick and Frack relationship also incorpo-

EDIE BASKIN

EDIE BASKIN

Opposite: Dan as Irwin Mainway, crass entrepreneur, demonstrating new toy for kids, Johnny Space Commander mask; this page, top, the Czech Brothers Festrunk (Dan with Steve Martin) try to pick up "foxes" Gilda, Laraine & Jane.

rates elements of Abbott and Costello, antic patrolman Gunther Toody and Francis Muldoon of *Car 54 Where Are You?* TV fame, and a slightly stoned out Huntley and Brinkley.

Usually Belushi pretends to be blasé about Aykroyd's ribbing, but actually he revels in it. When Belushi is in an especially ornery or obsessive mood, Danny will creep along behind his corpulent comrade as they go through the day's activities, Aykroyd making loudly whispered explanations to onlookers like, *"Ssssh! The Thing is feeding!"* or, *"Behold, the Bear Man rests!"*

Belushi usually gets his licks in when Aykroyd isn't around—or when Danny's manic meticulousness backfires. "Here's the difference between us," John tells me later. "See, I never carry any ID, no driver's license, no passport when I travel, nothing. I couldn't care less. He always carried this big ID wallet, big as a purse, that he kept *chained* to his belt at all times. When he lost it I was laughing my ass off.

"He's Mister Careful and I'm Mister Fuck It.

I can't always figure him out; but whenever I'm around him I feel safe."

Actually Aykroyd is that and more, a batch of contradictions forged into a willful, dependable whole. But it wasn't always thus.

"My brother and I were hellions," Aykroyd says with a smile, picking at some leftover Japanese food scattered upon the room-service cart. "Incorrigible. All through school there were discipline problems with me particularly. I was a chatty little sort. The Fat Mouth in primary school. I've had a solid relationship with my father for years, even though there was à lot of corporal punishment there as a kid. Many belt whippings. We deserved it.

"You know how parental units are," he laughs. "My mother always had friends that she wanted me to see: these prim, nice little girls and correct-speaking guys. Eventually I found out these people were as delinquent and corrupt as I was. When you got down in the basement with them, they wanted to crack open a bottle of whiskey same as you."

Young Dan Aykroyd's first memorable brush with alcohol and delinquency occurred while he was in the seminary.

"One night we blew down to Massena, New York, near the Thousand Islands area, 'cause you could drink in New York at eighteen. But, uh, I was fourteen at the time. We bought this vodka, went into this field, and suddenly out of nowhere there was the ringing of shotgun shells. This farmer was running us off his land. So we jump back into the car and go to a hamburger joint. The fucking place filled with cops with their guns out and they grab us, take us down to jail. My parents thought it was over for me at that point."

They weren't far wrong. Shortly thereafter the seminary superiors tired of his "late-night vandalism, skipping mass, fucking off" and expelled him. He completed his high-school education in a coed Catholic school in Ottawa.

"My friend, there were much better men than me there to serve the Lord," he clucks. "We were all supposed to be little angels, little priests. But we'd put on our polka dot mod shirts, Wildroot creme oil, Beatle boots, and *cut loose.*

"In my main years in high school I was a flattop, butch-waxed, with no hair on the sides. Then I got into the Beatle phase; went through a light greaser phase and then finally long and unwashed—my hair *and* me."

And things got even hairier when Aykroyd reached college. "He and his friends—a gang called the Black Top Vamps—lived in old houses in Ottawa and it was just like *Animal House,*" says brother Peter. "They used to have parties and they'd go into the same shopping plaza every weekend with beer cartons, order filet mignon from the meat counter, slip them past the girl at the cash register and leave."

During this period the multifaceted Aykroyd played harp in several bands, notably Top Hat and the Downtowners.

"In its day, the group was like Dan Hicks

and His Hot Licks," says Danny. "I was into jazz first, Art Blakey, Erroll Garner, Mingus and Thelonius Monk. Then I started listening to blues and stuck with that. I don't really have broad tastes for modern music and I don't like disco too much, although 'Le Freak' by Chic is nice. My tastes are narrow, see. The first record I ever bought was *Hymns of the Army, Navy and Air Force.*

"But I liked playing in the Downtowners. I had a great friend in the band who was also an acid dealer. He always had bundles of hundred-dollar bills."

Apparently Aykroyd has had many such companions.

"The guy who put my life on a different path was my friend Dave Benoit. I love him dearly. He's a low-class merchant seaman—by his own admission. He turned me on to music, let me smoke my first joint, introduced me to a woman I had a little thing with when I was fourteen, and awakened me to the hip scene around '67 in Ottawa, this whole underworld I never knew existed. I decided I was dropping out and I've never looked back.

"The most profound night of my life, the turning point, was the night we went out in a stolen Cadillac with this guy called Ray the Green Beret. Ray was an ex-Green Beret who'd ripped this Cadillac off in Wisconsin and driven it north. I got high that night and met George the Thief, a crazy French Canadian, and ultimately I just started to hang out with these people.

"'*I yam a teef! I yam a teef!*' That's what George used to say, and that's all he used to do. You could always obtain any amount of fenced goods through him. I still see these people and probably will associate with them for the rest of my life."

Up until his college years, Aykroyd's dad did his best to divert his sons from a life of slovenliness and iniquity. "Industry—the old man was big on that, ya know?" he tells me. "I mean, for my twelfth birthday I got an electric lawn mower to do the lawn for my father. That was my present, with a bow on it and everything. Thank you very much, Dad, thank you *very much.*

"He had me out at thirteen, working. I worked as a warehouseman, a brakeman on a railway. During college I drove a Royal Mail truck. But I'm glad I did that blue-collar stuff. My father would pull strings for me. He always knew somebody somewhere and he'd hear about these weird jobs.

"I was a dial reader on a runway load-testing unit. I almost got killed one night at Toronto International Airport when a DC-8 took off and grazed the station wagon I was riding out to the site in. Man, it was heavy.

"The best job was one I took at seventeen in the Northwest Territories surveying a road. We were up in an isolation camp. It was heavy work but you could really enjoy the territory: the crows, white wolves, bears. We used to skin and roast ground squirrels on a stick and they tasted just like chicken. A fabulous little rodent. *Sooo* tasty. Whenever we were low on Spaghetti-Os we had no choice.

"I was up there in the wilderness with Indians: Cree, Blackfoot. Jeeze, it was a great summer. But it gets tense up there. The drinking was heavy. Mounties up there don't wear uniforms 'cause it's so far north nobody's gonna check on them. And there was this one young cop up there, a real eager beaver we'd see when we'd come in and drink with the Indians and local townspeople of Fort Simpson. This young cop, he'd dance with the Indian girls and hang out, wearing a corduroy suit and cowboy boots, and then half an hour before the dance was over, he'd go back to the RCMP detachment and put on his hat, bring a fuckin' paddy wagon back and bust the drunken Indians, *everybody.* He was just the worst. You know, actors and sheriffs, for centuries, have never gotten along."

With one notable exception.

"My buddy Marc O'Hara and I, for three years we ran the best bootleg booze joint that there ever was in Canada, the Club 505 in Toronto. This was on Queen and River streets, and some of the cops we met on that beat who'd come in and ask us what we were doing we still know today as friends.

"You could drive by on the street and look in and see all these people drinking and we were just protected and covered for three years by whatever karmic umbrella.

"I'd work at Second City at night and run the bar from one a.m. on. The 505 Club was completely furnished with old Forties-style couches and plush armchairs, a barber's chair. All scavenged and scrounged. We slept in lofts above whatever crept on the floor at night. It bordered on serious squalor at times.

"I remember I went down to the 505 once to take a shit. I sat down on the toilet and I was reading and I heard this scrabbling in the bottom of the bowl, this slushing-about. I thought, 'Must be flushed water going from the back of the tank into the plumbing system,' so I continued reading. Finally I looked down into the excrement that lay there and a rat was clawing its way up the side of the bowl, its jaws just *inches* from my vital parts.

"Lorne [Michaels, executive producer and creator of *Saturday Night Live*] and I had met at the 505 one quiet night when it wasn't open. He sat in the barber's chair by the fish tank and he talked about what he hoped the show would be."

When the cast was being chosen Michaels asked Danny to come to the auditions.

"I came down from Canada with this guy named Dan Hennesey who was working on *Coming Up Rosie* with me. We were gonna sing this song we'd written about Jimmy Hoffa for Lorne, but the audition was a real cattle call with 200 people. I spent a minute and a half in the room, saying hello to Lorne, and then a friend of mine and I took off to California. Lorne called me and said, 'Come on, ya gotta come back!' And that was it."

"It's always been my understanding," I object, "that Michaels was very skeptical as to whether he could tame you and Belushi."

"Well Lorne *wasn't* sure about John and I," Danny admits. "I met John in Second City, and we were a little cocky and thought we didn't need it [the show]. I was cutting out a good wedge in Canada and I had the bar going, which was important to me and quite prosperous. Life was comfortable."

Since that time, life for Aykroyd has remained comfortable, although he's sometimes made things uncomfortable for the higher-ups at NBC.

According to one of his writing collaborators, Aykroyd got pretty infuriated with an NBC executive in 1977 for not paying him as both an actor and a writer for his work on a *SNL* special. "Danny took it as a point of honor; he was always fighting the NBC people. So what he did—he was *angry* at them—was get nails and paint and stuff, and outside of this guy's office and door he nailed and printed stuff onto the wall which had references to the cabala, psychic numbers and stuff. The phrases he made up were the things that some subway psycho would scrawl on a wall.

"He must have worked for hours on this thing; the place was a mess. He really terrified that whole wing of NBC. And, really, it was just Danny figuring out what would scare people the most. God, I thought it was funny. I'd like to see him to do more of that kind of thing on the show. It was a monstrous practical joke."

"It was *not* a joke," Belushi later tells me. "They took $400 out of his paycheck—money he should have gotten—and didn't tell him beforehand. You don't do that with Danny. So being a really smart guy, he thought up this thing to fix 'em real good, and he wrote, 'I am the Devil, I am Beelzebub!' on the walls in red and all this very satanic stuff, just to freak them out. And it worked. He was mad at them and they deserved it.

"They couldn't understand why he would do something like that, but I could understand it. And they'll think twice," John sniggers sardonically, "before they take money out of *his* pocket again."

Another thing Belushi says he can understand is Aykroyd's unfrivolous interest in UFOs, mysticism and psychic phenomenon.

"When Danny and I drive cross-country, we always look for UFOs, and I've gone up to his dead grandpa's farmhouse with him to wait for his ghost. Danny said he had seen it before, and I believe him. We used to turn the lights off and wait. He said it started as a green glow...."

"My grandparents used to have séances," says Peter Aykroyd, "and our dad passed the interest along to Danny and me. In our house it was just something that was accepted as viable. We never had séances but they were very regular at my grandparents' house when Dad was in his twenties, and my grandfather had a whole accounting on paper of his séances, who came through and what was said. He had photographs of the people who appeared in the room.

"Our father still has an interest in mysticism. He definitely rubbed it off on us, and we were always very interested."

As to the notion that his older brother is an excitable boy, Peter merely feels that Danny's sensitivity is miscomprehended.

"He's a real approachable guy in his own way, you know? And he really creates relationships quick with people because he has a way of, like, interrogating, like a cop. When you answer all the questions about yourself, you suddenly get the feeling: 'Gee, he knows me, therefore I know him.'"

The more one knows about Daniel Edward

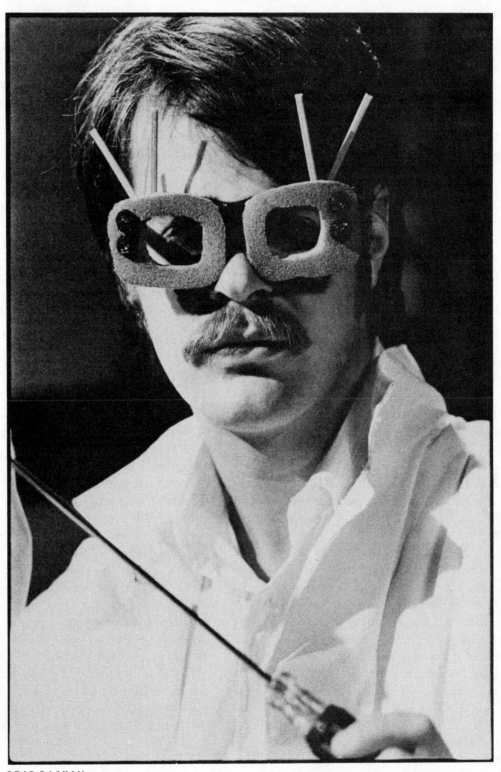

EDIE BASKIN

Aykroyd the more it seems there is to know. Beyond each door in his makeup is another door, slightly ajar, that opens on a room leading to still another. The complexity of the man is staggering. Yet certain constants emerge from the fabric of his web-footed personality.

"I don't want to wax poetic about it," says Michael O'Donoghue, "but Danny gives you a real solid bounce. You feel he's really there and you can trust him."

"You wonder how everybody on the *Saturday Night Live* show seems to handle the pressure," Peter Aykroyd muses, "and Danny, he seems to deal with it like it's a nine-to-five gig: 'I walk in, I write my scenes, I do my thing, I get out.' When things get bigger, as with the *1941* film, I think he can deal with it because *1941* is just another clear-cut job. He sets his own timetable.

"Now he's starting to get recognized on the street, he's going to become a personality. In the ego sense, I think he can handle it real well; no problem. I guess people don't handle stardom because of some insecurity and he's pretty damn secure."

LATER IN THE EVENING I FIND myself sitting with Aykroyd in a quiet room on the top floor of Jefferson Starship's Airplane house in San Francisco as the New Year's Eve bash for the Blues Brothers begins to wind down. Danny is ruminating on a variety of subjects ranging from the invention of stucco paint, to the genius of car customizer Ed "Big Daddy" Roth and the flaws in the design of the NASA space shuttle, when his clever, curly-haired girlfriend, *Saturday Night Live* writer Rosie Shuster, ambles by. They speak briefly, and when Shuster departs Danny's talk turns to their relationship.

"Lorne [Michaels] and Rosie were married," he volunteers softly, "and—it's so strange—I go out with Rosie and have been for a while.

We're an 'in-house' group over at *Saturday Night* and, hey, I'm a hetero, ya know? When you spend twelve, thirteen hours together at a stretch writing that show, there's a physical attraction and a magnetism sometimes.

"You know what I mean," he says, nudging me playfully, and then turns to watch Rosie bound down the stairs to the second floor. "She's a good girl," he says, a little sad. "Life is a funny deal."

I am finally beginning to feel that I understand this Man of a Thousand Faces when he dons another one, abruptly shifting the topic of conversation to, of all things, crime.

"I took a lot of crime-related courses in college," he says stiffly, as I gulp from a bottle of champagne offered by a passer-by.

"I took a course in criminology, one in correctional policy, one in deviant psychology. It was a program heading toward a career in prison classifications. I worked for the penitentiary service as one of my summer jobs and wrote a thick manual—it may still be in use—on personnel placement for the solicitor general's facility in Ottawa.

"There's always gonna be crime; I mean, I *know* this. I saw the graphs for Canada over a period of ten years on the flow of prisoners and recidivists and there's no bell curve there. It's either a holding pattern or it gradates upward."

"Why is that?" I ask, still uncertain why he brought it up.

"It's simple," he says with the curt detachment of a prison warden. "It's Robert K. Merton's sociological theory; probably the most tangible bit of knowledge I've gotten from *all* my training: the theory of 'illegitimate means.' When people from low-income groups see a TV or a car advertised they usually don't possess the legitimate means to get it. Frustrated, they have to resort to illegitimate means; so they pull a cheap job, a heist, a robbery, maybe break a pete."

"A pete?"

"Yeah, a pete, a safe."

"Hmmm," I mull, beginning to wonder whether Aykroyd isn't trying out a new character on me. "Did any of this data/experience rub off on you?"

"On me? Well, I'll say this. My grandpa was a Mountie, and I have my experiences through research, among other things. I've noticed that in street crime, you have officers always forcibly restraining suspects that are being arrested. But in any situation where the criminal has a *skill,* as with a good pete man, there's a moment between the arresting officer and the skilled criminal when it's all over and he's been caught and everything relaxes. There's *no* tension any longer; they light cigarettes and share a smoke.

"At this level, you see, they're kindred spirits; part of the same huge business. It's an art, a *craft,* an industry like any other!

"But *say,*" he says with a sudden smile, offering me a joint as he slips on a pair of Ray-Ban No. 5022-G15 sunglasses. "So what did you think of the way we played 'Jailhouse Rock' tonight?"

EDIE BASKIN

At left, Blues Brother Elwood on the harp with Joliet Jake. Note Elwood's Ray-Ban No. 5022-G15 sunglasses. He seems to bear a strange resemblance to Dan Aykro—naw, that's crazy.

EDIE BASKIN

LARAINE
Newman

BY
MARYANNE
VOLLERS

LARAINE NEWMAN STROLLS into a party at the Jefferson Starship mansion with a stumbling-drunk Bill Murray on one arm and a cloth satchel on the other. Murray immediately heads for the bar and Newman plops down in a corner chair, alone, and starts digging through her bag. She takes out a deck of cards and carefully spreads them out on the glass-topped table in front of her.

It's an hour before New Year's 1979, and the old San Francisco Victorian house is starting to fill up with rock stars and writers and friends of the band. Most of the crowd is gathered around a TV that's showing a live broadcast of the Blues Brothers and the Grateful Dead at the Winterland. Murray, who by now has become a happy public menace, occasionally stops by to say a few words to Laraine, and a couple of women sit down to chat for a moment. But she

EDIE BASKIN

rarely looks up from her cards, and she never moves out of the chair.

Laraine Newman, star of *Saturday Night Live,* passed the New Year playing solitaire.

OH, GOD! HOW'D YOU KNOW that?" she moans, covering her mouth with two bony hands. "Yeah, sometimes I do that at parties." She touches her face, then runs her fingers through her long auburn hair as if she's realizing for the first time that people can actually see her—even when she wants to be invisible. "I'm real shy and I don't like being approached by strangers."

Laraine Newman is sitting in the spare, immaculate kitchen of her West Side Manhattan apartment, drinking tea and picking at an English muffin. Even though it's early evening this is the first time she's eaten all day. "Ugghh, I must have had some bad pastries last night. I've been throwing up and I've had the runs ever since," she says, rubbing her stomach. "I must look a wreck."

Actually, even though she's a little washed-out from the food poisoning, she looks beautiful. Her face is much softer than it appears on screen, with large hazel eyes and a delicate mouth. The lower lip droops slightly, giving her a permanent look of sadness and vulnerability. The effect is exaggerated by her 5'4" body that weighs about ninety-five pounds.

"I've always been skinny," she says. "I'm trying like hell to put on weight." She eases herself out of her chair and plucks a giant vat of weight-gain powder out of the cupboard. "I mix this with bananas and milk every morning, but I keep losing anyway." She looks down at the pajama pants drooping around her legs. "But I'm real strong. I may not look it, but I am."

She sits down and lights a cigarette. "Once I weighed 108 pounds. That was back in 1971 when I was studying mime with Marcel Marceau in Paris. We had six-hour-a-day workouts doing ballet and fencing and acrobatics, it was great . . ." She stops for a moment, then her face twists in horror. "God! That was *eight years ago.*"

LARAINE NEWMAN, WHO turned twenty-seven a few weeks ago, can't imagine doing anything except acting. "It's the only thing I equipped myself to do," she says. "I've always been headed this way."

She was born and raised in Los Angeles, California, one of four kids in an upper-middle class Jewish family. Her father manufactured quilts, and her mother "did what a lot of Beverly Hills matrons do," including helping

EDIE BASKIN

Opposite, Laraine as Lina Wertmuller; this page, left, Laraine with Gilda and Jane, the "NBC Chimes," opening the show; below, on a lineup.

build the Westwood Playhouse, a theater near U.C.L.A.

Laraine Newman went to Beverly Hills High School where she was a poor student, but "threw herself completely into drama." After all, she didn't have much else to do. In a social scene dominated by surfers and the golden-skinned children of movie stars, Laraine was a bit . . . different.

"Oh, God, it was the most boring ugly-duckling story ever," she says. Not only was Laraine Newman painfully skinny, she had terrible acne and scoliosis, or curvature of the spine, that put her in a back brace for two years. ("It usually causes hunchback," she says. "I'm still a little uneven. It's been arrested, but not cured. One side has a shoulder blade and the other doesn't.")

Laraine Newman never had a date in high school. "But I never knew what I was missing," she remembers. "I was *involved*. I directed and cast the first improvisational show ever done in Beverly Hills High. It was probably the first time 'shit' was said on that stage."

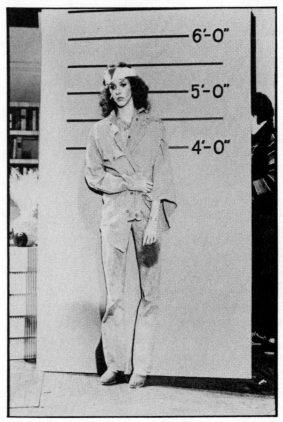

EDIE BASKIN

Left, as the Playboy Femlin, opening the show hosted by Hugh Hefner; opposite, in rehearsal for "The Coneheads."

EDIE BASKIN

After graduating in 1970, Newman had no intention of going to college, so she left home to study with Marceau in Paris. When that was over she came back to LA where she spent a couple of semesters at Cal Arts ("that was real bogus") and in 1972 joined the Gary Austin Workshop, where she studied acting and improvisation. Within a year and a half the workshop grew into an improv company called the Groundlings.

Gary Austin, who still directs the Groundlings, started her off using monologues to hold the audience's attention during set changes in the performance. "She objected to that strenuously," says Austin, "but she did it anyway, and she turned into one of the highlights of the show. Laraine would come out four or five times a night fully dressed each time as a different character, and she'd talk to the audience. The amazing thing was that we were in a thirty-seat theater, where the front row was probably two feet from the stage, and at the end of the evening a lot of people would go home not knowing that all the characters were

Laraine. She was so different each time."

One night in late 1974, Lorne Michaels and Lily Tomlin caught Laraine's act and decided to use her in Tomlin's TV special that Michaels was producing. Michaels was so impressed with her work that he asked Newman to move to New York to be part of a new show he was developing called *Saturday Night Live.*

Gary Austin cried when Michaels told him he was hiring Laraine Newman.

Now Newman has four seasons of *Saturday Night Live* under her belt. She's also played Teenage Louise in the 1978 film *American Hot Wax* and starred in a 1979 television special called *Bob and Ray & Jane, Laraine and Gilda.*

The menagerie of characters Newman developed at the Groundlings has expanded to include Connie Conehead, Lina Wertmuller, Barbara Streisand (Oh, my man I love him so, but not like I love *me"),* the model Vanessa Lake, a marauding Killer Bee, and Z. Jones, the luded-out rock critic on Weekend Update. But one of her best characters is probably her oldest, Sheri the stewardess. Her appearance on the

Godfather Group Therapy bit is a *Saturday Night Live* classic:

Elliott Gould, as a pipe-smoking therapist, perches on his desk and tries to coax Vito Corleone (played by John Belushi) to act out his feelings about his son's murder. Laraine Newman is Sheri, wearing a black minidress and a long blonde wig that she keeps teasing with a pink comb. Sheri constantly interrupts Vito's monologue, chirping, "Gaahyee, Vito, yer blocking." Finally Vito stuffs an orange rind in his mouth, lurches around grunting like a sow, then grabs his chest and collapses at Sheri's feet.

The therapist turns to Sheri and asks calmly, "How do you feel about what Vito just went through?"

Sheri takes a deep breath then starts jabbering like a parakeet on speed. "Well, I thut it was really beautiful, and like I can relate to the kind of changes Vito was going through. Cuz I went through the same thing when I was deciding to be a stewardess. I'm not kidding, man, ya know. My friends kept asking, "Gaahyee, Sheri, why do you want to be a stewardess?' I mean like I had to get super reflective and ask myself, well, gaahyee, Sheri, why do you want to be a stewardess? And you know I realized it's cuz (she rocks back and forth with a big grin) I love people. I really do, I love to serve 'em and help them try to fall asleep sitting up and everything. (Suddenly serious) Also I really had to get out of Encino man. I am not kidding . . . So I knew I had a bitchin' bod and a good personality so I just left town and I became a stewardess, you know, and I grew so much emotionally, I couldn't believe it. Cuz like I went back to Encino and everybody seemed so immature, it was unreal. You know doctor, I think Norman Mailer was right. You can't go home. . . ."

"Sheri is like those L.A. chicks I knew when I was growing up," says Laraine Newman. "They became secretaries, receptionists and stewardesses," (she launches into Sheri's cheerful-twangy dialect) "And they're real concerned about their looks and stuff." She laughs and lights her tenth cigarette of the hour.

Although Laraine Newman admits she recognizes a little of her own personality in Sheri—sometimes she slips and starts to *sound* like the character—Newman's not so concerned about her looks and stuff, at least not onstage. In fact the former ugly duckling is willing to make herself hideous—just to get a laugh. When she plays Lina Wertmuller, Laraine puts on a short wig, dark lipstick and gruesome white sunglasses.

But costumes are only props; Laraine New-

IRA RESNICK

man's genius is her ability to completely absorb her characters, then communicate them with her body and voice. Newman could be Lina Wertmuller without the wig and glasses—all she needs is a shrug of her shoulders, quick gestures with her cigarette, and, most important, the husky inflections of her voice.

"I have no idea what Lina Wertmuller sounds like," she says. "I've never met her. And when I do her, I'm not playing an Italian accent, I'm doing a French Canadian accent, cause I figure no one the fuck knows anyway. It's just an eccentric sound."

"Laraine's just brilliant at taking her characters through any accent or any dialect from a part of the country," says Gilda Radner. "Sometimes I'll get her to drill me on an accent, cause mine always turn out Swedish.

"Laraine's also a great physical comedian," Radner continues. "She can make her body do these really funny things. Once we did a piece called 'Little Known Talents of the Not Ready For Prime Time Players' and she did this chicken possessed by the devil! But most of

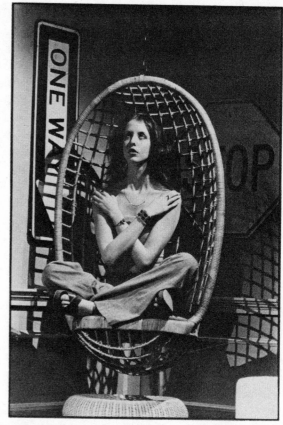

EDIE BASKIN

EDIE BASKIN

*A*bove, Laraine as hippie nymph; at left, backstage with friend Gilda; opposite, in bee costume, sipping pollen from a rose; page 137, as Sherri Norwalk, the secretary, in a sketch on Elizabeth Ray.

these things we just do around the office to make each other laugh."

Tracy Newman, Laraine's thirty-six-year-old sister, who teaches at the Groundlings and coached Laraine at the Gary Austin Workshop, remembers Laraine's first skit with the company. "There was an exercise we used to do called 'deformities' where you put two people on stage and every line one says has to make the other more deformed. Like one would say, 'Oh, you're walking nicely since you lost your leg,' and the other would have to hobble around on one leg. It goes back and forth until both actors are lying on the floor and can't move. Laraine had the guts to get right up there the first time. And she was hilarious!"

"Tracy was a great teacher," says Laraine Newman. "She's responsible for a lot of my success. Tracy and Gary Austin forced me to try new stuff that was foreign to me, and it really made me grow."

When I ask if working with Lily Tomlin has influenced her style, Laraine begins to speak very carefully, "No one has influenced me. I do have my idols, like Madeline Kahn and Richard Pryor, but they haven't affected my work. I guess the natural assumption is that Lily Tomlin influenced me, but she hasn't either. I didn't even *like* her on *Laugh-In*. I didn't like her until her Broadway show, which knocked me out. Still, she's not to my taste. She's not hard enough for me."

Richard Pryor's material is hard enough for Laraine Newman. But his act, which depends heavily on the use of obscenities, always seems watered-down on television. I ask Newman if she'd feel less restricted if she could say or do anything she wanted on the air.

"No, it's not important to me," she says. "Pryor can use that language because it's natural for him, and it works. For a lot of artists it's just a cheap laugh.

"The only time I felt inhibited by censorship was when I wanted Sheri to say 'pissed off.' And I couldn't. But I said it anyway, without telling anybody that I would. And Herminio Traviesas, one of NBC's censors, called Lorne Michaels and said, 'We're gonna put you on seven-second delay, which means technically you're not live.'

"So I called Traviesas and said, 'Look, I did it on purpose—it didn't just slip out. And I don't want to jeopardize the rest of the show because of it. And I'll never do it again. (Her voice becomes a pleading croak, like someone is stepping on her chest) Puhleeeeaaase, Mr. Traviesas, *please* don't put us on seven-second delay.' So he didn't.

"But 'pissed off!' Really! I don't think that's such a harsh term. But there are those who do."

Although censorship doesn't seem to bother her much, there are those who feel that the very format of the show inhibits Laraine's work. Each scene on *Saturday Night Live* is carefully scripted—there usually isn't enough time for the actor to get into a character, to run

EDIE BASKIN

with it and explore its natural limits. And Laraine Newman rarely writes her own scenes.

"Laraine did all her own writing at the Groundlings," says Gary Austin. "Her characters were richer there. On *Saturday Night* she's a little more surfacy, more hurried, a little more one-dimensional. I think the best writer for Laraine is Laraine. Whoever's writing for her now is not fully exploring what she can do."

Laraine Newman doesn't complain about it much, but it's easy to see how the lack of control bothers her sometimes. She remembers when her rock-critic character, Z. Jones, was delivering a monologue about Elvis Costello, and the writers made her say, "Wow, man, I hope I get this out before the ludes kick in."

"They were saying, put it in, it'll get a laugh!" she remembers "I thought it was a cheap laugh. But I gave in and said it anyway."

"Sometimes the writers come up with real prep-school, sick humor, you know. And a few of them . . . it's like, hating women, fear and loathing of women . . ." She stops short and looks down at my tape recorder. "But that's another tape."

When I ask about how women are treated on *Saturday Night Live,* and how she feels about the fact that only last year she had to share a dressing room with Jane Curtin and Gilda Radner while the men on the show had individual cubicles, she waves her hand in front of me to brush off the questions. "That's gossipy stuff," she says. "I don't want to talk about it. I get along with everyone."

One thing can be said about the cast of *Saturday Night Live;* they're tremendously protective of each other. There's a lot of talk about the "family atmosphere" on the show. And even though there are occasional rumors of private squabbles and jealousies—nobody talks about it publicly. It's kept in the family.

The women on *Saturday Night Live* seem particularly loyal and supportive.

"Laraine is my *sister,*" says Gilda Radner.

"There's this incredible thing on the show—that after four years there's a very strong love and respect between Laraine and Jane and me. Maybe it's because we just sit around for *hours* on the set. We've told each other stories about every dog we've ever owned, everything that happened in school.

"Laraine and I are paired up on the show a lot; we've gotten real proficient at being bookends. When we're doing a piece together where we have to do things in unison, I always say to Laraine, 'You just do what you do, and I'll copy it exactly.' "

Gilda Radner pauses a moment. "You know, I really love Laraine. But oddly enough, we don't hang out much with each other off the show. We spend so much time there, I guess we realize it's the healthiest thing."

LARAINE NEWMAN HAS JUST finished lunch at the Museum Cafe, a noisy Manhattan restaurant where we have our next meeting. "Sorry if I've been a little foggy," she says. "I'm not used to being up this early."

The waitress comes over for the fifth time to ask Laraine if everything's okay, and Newman surrenders her half-eaten cheeseburger. "It was real good, honey," she tells her. "But I just couldn't finish it. I tried."

When I open my wallet to pay the check she spots my press card and squeals, "Ooooohhh, who's this little person in the picture?" Suddenly she's using the voice of a precocious nine-year-old. "Hi! I'm from ROLLING STONE!" she squeaks. Thanks Laraine.

We take a cab back to Laraine Newman's apartment building where we have to walk through a voluptuous gothic lobby to get to the elevator. "Randolf Hearst built this place," she says. "Looks like a bordello, doesn't it? All these Catholic-repression red curtains."

Upstairs, Laraine Newman's living room is empty, except for two gray velvet couches dec-

EDIE BASKIN

orated with white pillows shaped like huge Quaalude tablets, inscribed with the word "Rorer." The walls are white, and the room is dominated by a huge window looking over the West Side Highway to the Hudson river. The apartment is quiet except for occasional traffic noises and the sound of Laraine's voice.

"I never really moved in here," she says. "I love New York, but I usually spend my time off in L.A. I don't care what anybody says about Los Angeles, it's a great city."

She settles into a couch and pulls her gray cashmere sweater around her shoulders. "I'm a second generation Californian," she says. "My father was born in L.A. before his family moved to Arizona, where they had a Brahman bull ranch."

"Our family's Jewish, but I never was in a temple until Kennedy was shot. California Jews are so assimilated they might as well be Presbyterians," she says. "And my father, you know, is *not* a jewboy. Like, he's got this phobia of cats, and once I brought a cat into the house, and he turned black with rage and said, 'You get that ornery varmint outta here!' And I went, *wait a minute,* Jewish fathers don't say 'ornery varmint!' "

Along with Tracy, Laraine Newman has an older brother Steven, 38, who's a lighting director for a rock band, and a twin brother, Paul.

"Paul designs clothing," says Laraine. She gives me a suspicious look, then leans down and shouts into my tape recorder, "But he's *not a fag!*"

"Paul's always been great at mimicking people. When we were real little he used to mimic Tracy's boyfriends and it would be so *accurate.* He was funnier than I was, and I always competed with him to get the stage."

Laraine's voice gets softer as she describes Paul. It's obvious she likes to talk about her brother.

"Paul and I have always been real close. Sometimes we could read each other's minds.

Like when we were four we used to have the same nightmare. It was about this creature called Go-Go the Dirt, and the only way to kill him was with a vacuum cleaner."

"Growing up with Paul was great for me, cause I learned what it was like to be close to a male. It's sort of afforded me a male point of view. I've always had good friendships with men. I like 'em."

Laraine Newman was always "best friends with the guys the other girls liked," throughout her dateless high school years. It wasn't until she was nineteen, after the acne cleared up and the brace came off, that Laraine had her first boyfriend.

These days Laraine Newman goes out with rock star Andrew Gold, and there are a lot of men out there who'd give anything to take his place. NBC receives a steady stream of love letters, sordid propositions and marriage proposals addressed to Laraine. When I tell her that a few of my male friends want me to give her their phone numbers, she laughs. But when I ask how it feels to be cast in the role of sex symbol, and to be desired by all these strange men, she is suddenly serious.

"It's kind of scary," she says. "I can't deal with it at all. All my life I wanted, more than anything, to be pretty, and now that people think I am, it's like . . ." She sits bewildered. "Once after a show I *felt* I didn't do too well, someone came up and said, 'You *looked* great!' And I felt, like YOU ASSHOLE! I wanted to perform great! I don't want to hear I looked great, that's a euphemism.

"I'm starting to understand the plight of beautiful women—they want to be thought of as intelligent. I never had a problem with *that* before. Beautiful women just aren't taken seriously. That's what Marilyn Monroe was all about. What they've been writing about her is so sad, but I believe it's probably true because (she whispers) I just *know what that was like.* I mean the girl was *alone,* and she lived on the telephone. I do the same thing because I'm alone here."

"You know, it doesn't take much to crumble into a pile of ashes if someone says, in any way, 'You're *ugly.*' Which happened all my life. It wasn't like *I'd* tell myself I was ugly. I was given the idea by other people. All my life I was teased for being ugly, you know how kids are, and it caused me a lot of anguish."

Laraine Newman spent a lot of her childhood watching horror movies on TV. She was always surrounded by a horde of neighborhood kids, who she'd mesmerize with monster stories. "I always identified with the monster, of course, since I felt so ugly myself. I felt sorry for Quasimodo, and I loved Frankenstein. Really *loved* him.

"God, I always watched *Twilight Zone,* oh, the *Zone!* And *House on Haunted Hill* scared the shit out of me. So did *Dracula.*"

Would she ever like to play a vampire, I ask.

"Oh, *yeah,*" she says. "In fact I've got some teeth. Want to see them?"

She runs into the bedroom and comes back with a handful of yellow fangs. "I had them made special to fit my teeth," she says as she slips one of them on to her canine. "Some of them are glazed to look like saliva, and some of them are matte. There!" She flashes a diabolical smile. During the rest of our conversation she bares her teeth from time to time, to illustrate a point about the art of horror, or just to make me nervous.

I ask Laraine Newman if anything scares her.

"Fans scare me," she says. "I can't deal with them. I know I'm gonna get slammed for this, but on a whole, they're *not nice.* I mean I hate it when someone comes up and says, 'Ey, you're *Laraine Newman!* Wow, man, remember that thing you did as Roseanne Roseanadanna . . .' and I go 'Yeeeaarrrgghh!'

"But then again, some kids are real intelligent and they'll come up and be real specific about things they like. And it's great when people you admire say nice things. Like once Woody Allen came up to me at a party and said, 'You're the best thing on that show.' Or when I was walking through the NBC lobby and I saw John Lennon coming out the door, and John goes, 'Hi, Laraine'–like he knew me. That was like (she throws her arms up and sings) 'My life is over! I can retire now!' "

So what happens when *Saturday Night Live* eventually goes off the air?

"I guess I'll go back to L.A. and try to make it as an actress," she says. "I've got a few possibilities in that direction, but I can't talk about them yet.

"I like doing movies, cause it's very rare that you get to do a part that sustains through a TV show. I enjoyed making *American Hot Wax,* although I think my performance was underwhelming."

Laraine Newman feels she'll be moving away from television, because her style and her material are not really accessible to a TV audience. "I don't think the people who watch TV would like what I want to do with my material," she explains. "I know that sounds really presumptuous, but I'm not saying (she puts on a snotty California twang) 'Eeeaaaoo, man. Like, Middle America, they're just not hip to my material.' I mean, they could indeed be, and still not like it.

"I never see anything in prime time I like, and if that's where they want to place me after *Saturday Night Live,* then I'd have to yield to a lot of restrictions. But I don't *have* to do it, and I *won't.* I mean, I'd rather buy a string of condominiums in Los Angeles."

The sun is setting on the Hudson River outside Laraine Newman's window. I thank her for her time, and just as she walks me to the door the phone rings.

"Oooohh, *hi* Aunt Charlotte! Happy birthday!" I hear her say as I quietly close the door.

EDIE BASKIN

THE Writers

EDIE BASKIN

Above, Rosie Shuster, Marilyn Suzanne Miller & Anne Beatts; at left, Herb Sargent; opposite, Al Franken & Tom Davis; p. 141, Michaels, Franken, Davis, Beatts, Aykroyd, Shuster, Schiller, (back row) Zweibel, Sargent, Doyle-Murray, Williams, Downey, Novello.

IRA RESNICK

EDIE BASKIN

IRA RESNICK

JEFFREY SWITZER

EDIE BASKIN

Opposite, top, Tom Schiller and Dan Aykroyd à deux; below, Alan Zweibel working with Jane Curtin; this page, left, Don Novello as Father Guido Sarducci; below, writers join with players, hosts & other staff members in "Celebrity Bingo."

EDIE BASKIN

LYNN GOLDSMITH

MICHAEL
O'Donoghue

BY TIMOTHY WHITE

WARNING : *The article you are about to read contains graphic descriptions of disturbing sexual practices and reckless violence. If there are older people with heart conditions in your household, or persons under psychiatric care, force this article upon them and make certain that they reread the especially unsettling sections. Do not allow children of an impres-*sionable age to leave the room without reading this article. If they are listless or sleeping, slap them. Wake them up. Give them some hot, black coffee.*

HE STANDS AT THE FULL-length window in his dismal living room, digs his boney white toes into a drab carpet the color of varicose veins and peers at the sunlight streaming past his West Village townhouse as if it were a quaint curiosity. My host is clad only in a wrinkled blue silk dressing gown covered with an odd flapping-wings design that merely hangs on his skeletal frame. Round dark sunglasses are firmly in place, accentuating the pale visage and further reducing a balding head no larger than a honeydew melon.

A cryptic smile passes across his thin lips and he steps to a low glass table to pour himself a goblet of wine. A tiny sip. Then he fixes me with the kelp-green gaze of a junkie jeweler.

"Questions?" he whispers.

I nod with a gulp and he moves to seat himself on the setee to my right, gently shooing away a nestled cat with the heel of· his hand—"GET AWAY FROM ME YOU SMARMY EGYPTIAN RUG RAT!"—before greeting me cordially: *"What? You didn't bring me any crystal meth! Well, you young dolt, don't expect much of an interview!"*

There is a burst of shrill laughter that rattles a houseful of grotesque brick-a-brack, and then he tries to calm us both with more blood-red bordeaux. It's always a pleasure to pass an afternoon with Michael O'Donoghue.

"Yes, there are a lot of things in life safer than comedy," he counsels with a smirking swallow. "But let's face it: when that sniper on the highway catches you in his sights, you're not thinking about statistics, eh?"

What, I wonder, was O'Donoghue thinking during his days (1970-74) as an editor of *National Lampoon,* and then as a writer-performer (1975-78) for *Saturday Night Live?*

"All along, I was thinking about anything that got a rise out of *me,*" he says with a wink. "I was looking at comedy with, not a jaundiced eye, but rather a *cancerous* eye. I once wrote an ad for *Saturday Night*—which *did not* get on the air—for a wonderful new product, Spray-on Laetrile. The ad started with a girl telling her boyfriend, 'Gee Jim, I'd love to go to the dance with you tonight but I can't. I have cancer.' And he says, 'Aww, come on honey! Haven't you heard about spray-on Laetrile? One little *psssst!* and you can kiss cancer goodbye!'

"But I never wrote or pandered to a market. I never made the stupid mistake of saying, 'I'm the New York sophisticate and I like this joke, but the pig masses in Crib Death, Iowa, will never understand it because they are such *filth.'* So I never did a Carol Burnett and wrote down to anyone."

The voice is overly calm, and modulated to simulate a gracious, albeit tentative, benevolence. He sounds like a mellow late-night FM disc jockey who slits little girls' throats each evening before he reports to work.

"Excuse me," says O'Donoghue, abruptly rising for more wine. "I think I forgot the question. Kitty Carlisle, do you want to field this one?"

THE *TO TELL THE TRUTH* INTER-jection is apt, reminding me of the general public's misunderstanding, fear and/or total ignorance of Michael O'Donoghue's unique knack for humor. He is perhaps best known as the originator of some *Saturday Night Live* skits depicting the possible reactions of the Mormon Tabernacle Choir, Tony Orlando and Dawn, and Mike Douglas, to having long steel needles thrust into their eyes. If your response to that kind of slapstick is an irate, "That's not funny, that's sick!" then you're at least getting the point, so to speak, of O'Donoghue's wanton wit.

A dropout from the University of Rochester, he first came to the attention of many while a contributor to the now-defunct *Evergreen Review,* in which he published bizarre, funny plays with names like "The Automation of Caprice" and also wrote a lurid comic strip parody named for its scantily clad superheroine, "Phoebe Zeit-Geist." The strips, later collected in a book, became a cult favorite and paved the way for a volume O'Donoghue authored in 1968 called *The Incredible, Thrilling Adventures of the Rock* ("It only took twelve minutes to read") whose sales were as slim as its storyline. Shortly thereafter, he slipped ("like swamp gas," according to colleague P.J. O'Rourke) into the Madison Avenue offices of the *National Lampoon* and there generated such broad strokes of parody as "Tarzan of the Cows," "Battling Buses of World War II" and "Underwear for the Deaf." When the *Lampoon* organization branched out into radio, records and books, Michael helped write the successful National Lampoon Radio Hour, co-created (with *Lampoon* editor Tony Hendra) the famous *Radio Dinner* album, and compiled an *Encyclopedia of Humor.* The last effort is perhaps best remembered for an entry called "The Churchill Wit," O'Donoghue's somewhat suspect mini-anthology of the jauntiest off-the-cuff quips by the late former Prime Minister of England:

> When the noted playwright George Bernard Shaw sent him two tickets to the opening night of his new play with a note that read: "Bring a friend, if you have one," Churchill, not to be outdone, promptly wired back: "You and your play can go fuck yourselves."

O'Donoghue rose to still-greater notoriety on *Saturday Night Live,* where he often appeared before the cameras in the sinister, sunglassed persona of "Mr. Mike," telling one of the "Least Loved Bedtime Stories" in which, for example, he reduced the hippity-hoppity antics of B'rer Rabbit to "random acts of meaningless violence." Incidentally, it seems his public comic sensibilities are identical to his private ones, and he confides with a bleak snigger that "There's no difference between Mr. Mike and me. He rose out of a dark emotional situation I was in. The sunglasses came out at the same time. It was a time of *snakes on everything.*"

Understandably, Michael is now remembered by his former *SNL* co-workers as "a certified nut-case," "an unbelievable hilarious, sick bastard" and "a true comic genius who will someday surpass Mel Brooks and Woody Allen."

It is the summer of '78 and, speaking of Woody Allen, O'Donohue has recently been asked by the celebrated fellow comic genius to play a small part in Allen's forthcoming motion picture, *Manhattan.* Things seem to be looking ever upward for Michael, who has just left *Saturday Night Live* to create three late-night specials in association with *SNL* producer Lorne Michaels. Working with a staff of young writers that includes Mitchell Glazer, Eve Babitz, Dirk Wittenborn and *Lampoon* alumnus Emily Prager, O'Donoghue has concocted a teleplay based on the lives of fashion models, a sci-fi horror epic about rampaging roaches entitled *The War of the Insect Gods,* and *Mondo Video,* a comedy takeoff on the sleazy 1960's oddities-of-the-world film documentaries.

O'Donoghue assures me he is genuinely thrilled that he is getting the chance to present his comic vision en masse and (hopefully) unadulterated to the nation's TV viewers. But, hey, Woody has just begun shooting *Manhattan* and it's not as if *everybody* gets invited to appear in one of Woody's films, and the man *did* win a shitload of Oscars last year for *Annie Hall,* so we shouldn't mind if Michael puts on a few airs and rhapsodizes just a *trifle* too much about his "crucial" role in Woody's next cinematic masterwork, eh?

"I can't talk about it! I can't!" he rages, stalking around the living room. "It's *impossible* for me to speak of it! I must respect Mr. Allen's confidence!

"But anyhow," he murmurs conspiratorially, suddenly crouching down next to me, "I play Diane Keaton's old boyfriend, Dennis, who's this asshole film director that Woody destroys to get to her. You know, there's always a paper tiger in these urban love affairs.

"I play the macho lead and—*get this*—I'm the male sex symbol. It's an interesting role because I've never been in a movie before and there was a heat inversion in New York the week we shot my scenes. I got terrible migraine headaches, so I had to take massive doses of Percodan. Consequently I can barely remember the lines, the shooting, anything, because it's all one narco haze."

Believe it or not, Michael's a charming guy who actually *likes* people—or several of them, anyway. As *Saturday Night Live* producer Lorne Michaels puts it, "Michael doesn't really believe that the human race is a lot of quivering scum. He just says he likes to feel that way because it gives him the nervous energy to get up in the morning."

"Life is not for everybody," O'Donoghue rules, and he admits he needs some extra encouragement to face the task. Over the years he's experienced a number of severe "emotional reversals" as he calls them, ranging from a brief ill-fated marital fling, to a glut of career disappointments. "So I got myself some dark glasses," he says, "and then once inside them I felt a lot better in the hidy hole and didn't want to come out for a long time. Tried to come out a couple of times while I was working for *Saturday Night* but I didn't make it. I couldn't stand the fluorescent lights in the NBC offices." The turning point came during a trip to Greece last August, when he took a shot at wearing clear glasses in order to best soak in the sights. Upon returning home, he tried to revert to his old ways but then misplaced his seaweed-colored shades. "I lost them, as the Fates would have it, and I'm not fucking with the Fates. I've studied Zen Buddhism and I'm like the bamboo tree—I bend with the wind. I'm not like the oak tree that breaks."

Not that he hasn't come close. Over the years there have been some real stress tests. See, there's another reason that Michael's brief appearance in *Manhattan* is so indicative of the man himself, and it's because all his crazed Percodan performances, the scenes in the cab and the Chinese restaurant that were probably his best stuff, ended up in the dumper. Michael O'Donoghue is a legend around the publishing and television industries not primarily for the things he's done that have reached the public eye, but rather for the er, *unusual* body of work that has never gotten past the Bowdlers, censors and other assorted arbiters of taste in this country. Needless to say, the expurgated material was pretty exotic fare. And then there's the slightly disturbing day-to-day behavior of O'Donoghue himself....

HELLO? YES, THIS IS MICHAEL. You wanna do another interview with me? The day after tomorrow? Why, that's my day of rest! Well, okay, I'll cooperate—but I'll be doing a lot of drugs; I'm not giving up *that* part of my Sunday.

"Besides, I've got a lot to talk about. I got an idea last night for a book of poetry called *Jesus May Love You, but I Think You're Garbage Wrapped In Skin.*"

I arrive at Michael's home on a frigid February afternoon and he admits me with a polite handshake and then a fatherly pat on the back.

"Have a seat old boy," he says, pointing to a green velvet couch across from the fire crackling away in his marble hearth. "Do you want some coffee? No? Well, I know you folks in the People's Temple are very strict," he deadpans, and then laughs heartily. Today he's wearing a baggy pair of brown corduroy pants that are belted tightly at his tiny waist, and a dark green pajama top with white piping. Shuffling around in slippers as he nips from a snifter of brandy, he seems nervous but eager to communicate.

"I have to get myself some coffee in a second," he mulls. "I took a Quaalude—half a Quaalude, which makes me honest. I don't have time to censor myself and I've always thought that truth is the ultimate lie. Human beings aren't capable of understanding it, quite frankly. It dazzles 'em. But you can ask me any question you want if you ask it honestly. Cock size, anything, I don't care." He smiles encouragingly.

I figured I'd begin by asking about his book of poetry but before I can, he insists I listen to a song he wrote at 4 a.m. this morning. As he hastens to recall it, I realize that he may have been up since then.

"Oh, this is a fucking beauty, this song! Let me see if I can put it together. It's called 'Blue Morphine.' I don't have a melody for it, so let me see if I can just talk it." He begins to recite the lyrics, occasionally lapsing into a surprisingly mellifluous croon.

> *I'm flying too close to the moon*
> *What is the light that dreams are lit with?*
> *Will it be over soon?*
>
> *Falling like angels cast from the sky*
> *Only blue morphine can teach us to fly*
> *Blue morphine*

"It goes on like this for a while," he bubbles, "and the last refrain comes after some really hot saxophone."

> *Falling forever, shadows and smoke*
> *Death is a lover, and love is a joke*
> *Blue morphine.*

"It's a bit on the negative side," he concedes with a beaming grin, "but when you make those major dream breakthroughs at four in the morning . . ." He cancels the thought, striving ahead. "You catch me at a very bruised time, because I've just gone through holiday dreams, and they leave you bruised and shattered. I had a dream one time, a real hot religious dream in which I was the baby Jesus, nude. Crucified above an altar. It was a kind of exhibitionist thing. And there was a lovely glowing gold altar in this gigantic cathedral but I couldn't see very far beyond it into the darkness. I could just hear the rustles of a few Italian women kneeling and paying homage. It was real nice."

Hmmm, well, that's certainly an interesting departure from the usual Irish Catholic guilt trip.

"I've always wanted to be Jesus," he says. "Let's face it, any Irishman has. A lot of my humor is like Christ coming down from the cross—it has no meaning until much later on."

Uhhh huh. On this sacriligious note, I decide to shift the conversation to O'Donoghue's own background, and he reveals that he underwent his fair share of suffering.

"A main influence in my life was the rheumatic fever I had when I was five," he begins, "and I stayed inside the house for a year. Now this *has* to be a negative turning point in a child's life, and so consequently I got into working in scrapbooks, stamp collecting, and so forth.

"Also, I developed a concept of 'others,' " he adds wryly. "For instance, you are one of the 'others' and the things that make you one of the others are that you don't feel the same things that I do, or even think the same things. I have a difficult time understanding others, their wants, their desires. It gave me a certain distance from which I could observe things. And I could read at that point, which is very bad. *Never* teach your child to read early. It just puts him at odds with the other kids."

Michael Henry O'Donoghue describes his background as that of a "weed bender." Born on January 5th, 1940, to Michael James Donoghue and the former Barbara Jane Zimmermann, he grew up in rural Sauquoit, New York, located some seven miles from Utica.

"My grandfather's name was O'Donoghue. He came to this country from Killarney and on the boat ride over he dropped the 'o' in the ocean, as the Irish are wont to say, but I put it back. My dad worked at a munitions plant, Remington Arms, during the war and then some white collar job in industry. He's very smart, jovial, with a good warm sense of humor. My mother is Welsh-German, a mean woman, and I get most of my search-and-destroy humor from her." Michael also has a sister, Jane, who is five years younger, with whom he is "not on good terms."

O'Donoghue admits he was "not a very popular kid" during his years at Sauquoit Valley Central High School, despite his involvement in the band, Chess Club, Library Club, baseball team, and especially the Dramatics Club (he was president).

"It was *not* a good period of my life," he recalls. "I was what was called a *nork,* a real creep, and the local girls certainly agreed, since I didn't have many dates. But the thing was that I was so damned bright that the other kids really couldn't keep me out of their lives.

"There was one boy, whose first name was Barton, who was pretty bright and even well-liked, and he would have been tough competition for me, but he drowned in the lake during the freshman picnic. I remember everybody in the class was watching the police dredge the lake, but we hadn't eaten yet and I was hungry. I grabbed a sandwich and the gym teacher started yelling at me, 'You monster, you *monster!*' Hell, I thought you could grieve and eat at the same time.

"I was very unhappy in high school but in college I wisely pretended to be another type of person—suave, confident, popular—and I got away with it!"

O'Donoghue majored in English in the University of Rochester, with a minor in Philosophy. At one point, he became immersed in oriental religions and says he has contemplated retreating to a monastery. After being kicked out of the University "for having a bad attitude," Michael migrated to California and attended both San Francisco State and the University of California at Berkeley. "I was leaning towards writing at that point," he recalls. "I started a magazine out there called *renaissance*—with a small 'r.' You know, one of those quaint literary rags with lots and lots of wood cuts. I ran it with a man called John Bryant; he'd published Charles Bukowski's poems and a lot of Gary Snyder's. Bishop Pike helped us out. Seriously. Very nice man. Gave us the key to the Episcopal Diocese office up on Nob Hill so we could type out the magazine there. We were always afraid he'd see what was in it. This was around 1960-61. It's sad about Pike's disappearance; they found his jockey shorts in the desert. Worst way to go I've ever heard of—no dignity.

"Around this time I was working for the *San Francisco Examiner* as a reporter trainee, worked in the wire room, did everything. I was fired 'cause I got into a fight in the city room. I grabbed a man's tie and pulled him across a desk. I was gonna hit him with a lead type bar, which really can leave some kinda *Tom and Jerry*-type indentation in the skull, but someone stopped me."

Shortly afterward, O'Donoghue returned to the University of Rochester in quest of a teaching degree, but quit after six months. He subsequently sold *Life* magazine by telephone, peddled shrubbery and then costume jewelry door-to-door, and worked as a credit manager for the Sherwin-Williams paint company. He also started a theater group called Bread and Circuses and worked as a disc jockey for WBBF-FM in Rochester, playing classical music and doing the hourly newscast, which he would often hideously distort by expanding the worst tragedy of the day—an earthquake, plane crash, etc.—into a long, grisly lead story, while scarcely mentioning any other occurrences.

Somewhere in there—he says he can't remember exactly when—he married a woman who already had three kids towards whom Michael had difficulty relating. In a matter of months the honeymoon and the marriage were over. After briefly dating a ballet dancer who he mentions "could totally bend over backwards and walk upside down without any clothes on like a crab," O'Donoghue fled to New York to live in the Village, where he toiled as a freelance writer.

O'Donoghue is close-lipped, to say the least,

about his marriage, simply stating that it was "traumatic." Several months later, some additional light is shed on the trauma while I'm sharing an Italian dinner at the fashionable Elaine's with Michael and his *Mondo Video* writing staff. When the talk turns to O'Donoghue's past, Dirk Wittenborn begins needling his boss about his "great affection for children," specifically O'Donoghue's "babysitting technique" during the short-lived period that he served as a stepfather.

"Come on, Mister Mike," says Dirk with a mischievous grin. "Tell us again how you used to get the baby boy to stop crying at night."

"Now *Dirk*," O'Donoghue cautions lightly with a queer twinkle in his eye. "Let's *not* go into that."

"Oh no, Mister Mike, you're not gettin' out of this one! What he used to do," Dirk tells me, "is that he would go into the baby's room each night with a loaded revolver ..."

"... and I'd fire off a round or two, always into the ceiling—just to get the little fella to quiet down," O'Donoghue minimizes with a nonchalant shrug. "Gave him quite a start but it always worked. How else was I supposed to stop the kid from crying?

"Say you want some of this pasta?"

A TRULY BRILLIANT WRITER, but a very difficult character" says *National Lampoon* editor-in-chief P.J. O'Rourke of his former co-worker. O'Donoghue was one of the original *Lampoon* editors when the humor magazine was founded in April of 1970. O'Rourke has great praise for Michael's talent, especially "his gift for combining the heroic with the banal, as in 'Tarzan of the Cows,' and his stellar sense of black humor."

But O'Rourke, like other staffers at the *Lampoon,* was often weirded out by O'Donoghue's explosive temper.

"He's a really proud guy and once he gets

mad—usually for a good reason—he gets mad out of all proportion to the stimuli," P.J. maintains. "And he stays mad forever."

"And Michael had a short fuse with everything. He'd do stuff like, if the office phones didn't work quite right—as office phones never do—well, one time he beat one of his phones to death with a cane, smashed it to pieces, then went over to the next office, picked up the phone, called the phone company and screamed, 'The phone is broken! Get right over here!' "

All of this is retold with great affection and an almost involuntary wistfulness. Compared to the *Lampoon*'s zany golden era (generally acknowledged to have been 1970-74), the legendary suite of offices now contains all the tumult of a sanitarium.

"Michael O'Donoghue was like the Cardinal Richelieu of the *National Lampoon;* he was definitely a guiding light," says a former editor of the magazine.

"When I left the *Lampoon* in 1974 I thought my next career move would be blowing off some of the editors' kneecaps," Michael rejoins, his voice rising. "I felt frustrated artistically and in other ways. I have a reputation as being a dangerous psychotic to work with because I'm so insistent on things being done my way, but I believe there are no sacred cows in comedy. All those snotty Harvard kids on the staff were afraid to go for the jugular. Hell, when *I* saw blood, it just excited me into a feeding frenzy. And happily, my voice—sex, violence and bad taste—became the magazine's editorial standard."

In retrospect, O'Donoghue places a higher value on his tenure there. "The *Lampoon* was hot in those days," he contends. "I think we could have kicked the hell out of the Algonquin Round Table the best day they ever lived. There was a long wait between quips at that damn potsy Round Table!"

During the O'Donoghue era, however, the

Lampoon editors seemed to spend most of their time kicking each other.

"The most difficult but also the most lovable writer was Michael," says Simmons. "And I still love him even though he won't talk to me. There was always fighting and wild outbursts from him and he was forever not talking to most of the other editors. And vice-versa. His writing was absolutely hysterical but it would attract some strange outside reactions.

"I'm in my office one day [April 6, 1972] and I get a call from the kid in the mailroom. He says, 'Mr. Simmons, there's a box here for Michael O'Donoghue and I don't like the looks of it.' So when O'Donoghue came in I said, 'Michael, let's open this box that just came in but let's open it *carefully.*' So we took it into his office, looked inside and there are these sticks of dynamite. He turns white, green, and orange. Then he picks up the phone and calls George Plimpton."

From there, Plimpton picks up the story. "Michael phoned me after he opened the dreadful package—I'm a demolitions expert, you see—and I told him that you could eat the dynamite and even hit it with a hammer and nothing could happen—provided the nitro glycerine had not leaked out and crystalized on the outside . . . which of course it had."

The building was quickly evacuated and Madison Avenue was closed off from 57th to 63rd Streets while a police bomb squad descended on the premises and removed the deadly package. The culprit turned out to be a pro-O'Donoghue prankster who mailed along the blasting caps several days later.

As Michael himself points out, his comedy is about "the tortured little shadow areas we hide from our friends." But he is not above exploiting *any* painful situation for the sake of a laugh.

"You want to know what an incredibly funny, sick, nutty guy O'Donoghue is?" Matty Simmons asks. "Let me tell you, Michael was once sitting in my office when his father called and explained that as the result of some unfortunate occurrence, Mike's mother had just had to have her toe amputated.

"His father said, 'Michael, there's something terrible I have to tell you.' And O'Donoghue said, 'Oh. What?' His father said, very sadly, 'Well, your mother lost her toe.' Michael paused for a second and then he said, 'Did you look for it behind the refrigerator?' "

As O'DONOGHUE MAKES HIMself some coffee in his cozy little kitchen, I roam around examining the glut of gimcracks in his apartment. Next to the fireplace in the living room stands an armless, battered little girl mannequin clothed in a misshapen dress who is gazing longingly out the window. Nearby is a large, stuffed bear wearing World War I-vintage aviation goggles. Crammed everywhere in this room and the adjacent den is a dusty array of stuffed game, including various fowl, foxes and a pinched-faced owl.

Michael wanders out of the kitchen and assists me in my reconnaissance.

"If that mannequin could talk . . . oh nothing," he says, dismissing the thought with a naughty laugh. He then directs my attention to the large glass cases lining one wall of the den.

"This is my rhinoceros collection," he says, pointing to several shelves packed with neat rows of identical miniature gray plastic rhinos. "And that's my dead aunt's tea service in there, lots of assorted flamingo figurines and stuffed specimens, and of course my collection of cheap perfumes." He reads off some of the names on the bottles: "Memories of Paris, Confetti, Sonata, Rapture, Ben Hur, Reckless, and Khus-khus—'As Used by Royalty.'

"They must have been dethroned royalty," says Michael, tapping at the last bottle. "This shit sells for ninety-five cents a half-pint."

I am contemplating the Frankensteinian

cluster of hatter's heads in the center of the case as Michael begins petting a nearby mummified ocelot. There is, somehow, a certain kinky poignance to the image, a notion not lost on O'Donoghue, who begins humming what sounds like a love ballad.

"What's that song?" I ask.

"Oh," he says, "it's called 'Cancer for Christmas.'"

"Huh?"

"Cancer for Christmas," he repeats, explaining that he wrote the song for the 1978 *Saturday Night Live* Christmas show. "I was booked to do it at the end of the program, standing in a tableau with fake snow falling behind me, but they wouldn't let me. I thought it was time we showed the dark side of Christmas. Hell, I've had a bunch of relatives *die* over the holidays. It was a true act of censorship." He tilts his tiny head to one side and sings his heart out:

> *Cancer for Christmas*
> *Blue lights on the Christmas tree*
> *Yule log burning on tv*
> *It's cancer for Christmas*
>
> *Here's a brand new Timex*
> *With a lifetime guarantee*
> *Don't kiss Mommy on the lips*
> *And don't sit next to me.*
>
> *Cancer for Christmas*
> *Plastic reindeer in the yard*
> *The cleaners sent a festive card*
> *With holiday greetings*
>
> *Santa's bringing sacks of morphine*
> *And some cigarettes*
> *Time to call the Bide-a-wee*
> *And give away your pets*
>
> *Play the tapes of "Silent Night"*
> *Sung by Patrice Munsel*
> *Wouldn't count on New Year's Eve*
> *It's time to say farewell*
>
> *We'll drink a cup of cobalt yet to auld lang syne.*

O'Donoghue's files are filled with outlandish material that the executive censors (Herminio Traviesas, Ralph Daniels and James Ottley) in NBC's Standards and Practices office have refused to okay for telecast. One such deletion was "Great Moments in Sports," a skit intended for the *SNL* show hosted by Fran Tarkenton, in which Bill Murray portrays Lou Gehrig delivering his heart-rending 1939 Yankee Stadium retirement speech. "A little while ago," Murray/Gehrig, tells the crowd, "I just found out that I have a fatal disease." Long pause. "Perhaps you didn't understand what I just said [*screaming*] I'M GONNA DIE!! A year from now all you dumb jerkoffs will be sitting here watching some stupid baseball game and I'll be *dead!!!"*

Murray/Gehrig quickly becomes hysterical and must be dragged, kicking and screaming, from the field. The segment was rehearsed and ready to air but the censors shook their heads: it ended up in the dumper. Likewise, a commercial for "Tarbrush, a toothpaste for Negroes"; a sketch in which Charles Manson (played by O'Donoghue) is carving his Halloween jack-o-lantern and begins stabbing the pumpkin repeatedly; and innumerable *Weekend Update* scripts, including the following rough gems:

> In an attempt to modernize its services, the Catholic Church has introduced something new into communion. In addition to dispensing the host, priests will now also dispense a "co-host," which symbolizes the body of Mike Douglas.
>
> What will the smart, fashionable woman be wearing this fall? From California comes the answer—a lovely floor-length Chowchilla coat. Chowchilla coats—made from the matched skins of twenty-six school children. They're not in the stores yet but it's only a matter of time.
>
> And in a related item, FBI Director Clarence Kelley denied rumors that the Bureau's entire investigation into Dr. Martin Luther King's death consisted of asking a Ouija board, 'Who shot the monkey?'

But O'Donoghue says his favorite expunged ribtickler was this proposed exchange between *Update* hosts Jane Curtin and Dan Aykroyd (which Michael slyly submitted under the pen name of Edith Wharton):

JANE: How long does it take to cook a baby in a microwave oven? Exactly 55 seconds per pound, claims Mr. Nils Nickleson of Median Strip, Arizona, who turned this small fry [baby projected on the screen behind her] into a small roast in only eight minutes and fifteen seconds.

DAN: Jane, to that let me simply add, 'Well done!'

"I tried to use a Jonathan Swift/Modest Proposal" argument with the censors on that last item," says Michael, "but they didn't buy the literary cross-reference."

Looking over the blue-pencilled material, I note that there are tasteless potshots and ethnic slurs of every stripe . . . but no gags against the Irish.

"Oh, the Irish are a little dim," O'Donoghue demurs. "Someday I want to return to my ancestral home to piss on the Blarney Stone, but basically the Irish are a race that is closer to the angels than to the apes."

When I ask whether his current project, *Mr. Mike's Mondo Video,* will be a fit network entertainment for the viewers at home, he changes the subject, promising a screening the following week of the raw footage of *"that* soufflé of trash."

A WILD HAIRED O'DONOGHUE, bent into a resolute slouch by the weight of his thick camel hair coat, is pacing the floor of a chilly loft in New York's East 20s, raging about a media skirmish that is in the offing.

"We give up nothing!" he bellows to his staff as he stalks amidst a bewildering sprawl of video equipment, a cock-eyed checkerboard of TV screens displaying various cold blue images of himself. This is the workshop where *Mr. Mike's Mondo Video,* three months in the writing and production stage, is finally being assembled. The air is electric with high-tension editing and bitter feuds as Michael's co-workers psyche him up for an impending meeting this afternoon with the NBC censors. It seems that

NBC harbors strong reservations about the bulk of the hour-and-a-half program. Objections center on such segments as "Celebrity Deformities" wherein Dan Aykroyd probes the skin of his webbed toes with a Phillips head screwdriver to prove the authenticity of his claim: "I am a genetic mutant." Also offensive to the NBC brass is "American Gals Love Creeps," a sequence in which heavily made-up vamps like Gilda Radner, Carrie Fisher, Margot Kidder, Deborah Harry, Laraine Newman, and John Belushi's wife, Judy Jacklin, whisper their uncontrollable affection for "guys who miss the toilet seat," "men who smell their fingers," "fellows who drink too much and can't get it up," and "guys who sneeze in their hands and wipe it on their pants," the sultry testimony culminating in the admission: "When I reach down and feel a firm colostomy bag, I know I'm with a *real* man."

Personally, I found *Mondo Video* to contain some of the most uproarious comedy material I have ever seen, full of O'Donoghue's sick-o flair, but certainly no more prurient or shocking—with the exception of a 1928 peep show entitled *Uncle Sy and the Sirens*—than such *SNL* staples as Dan Aykroyd denouncing Jane Curtin on "Weekend Update" as an "ignorant slut."

Nonetheless, the network is balking at broadcasting the show, presently four months late and $100,000 over its $275,000 budget, and O'Donoghue is fit to be tied.

"Damn those *cretins!*" he booms, "I took the 'Dancing Navel' routine out didn't I? I met them halfway! What were they expecting from me? *Porky Pig Takes a Trip?!* Well, here's what we do: if they try to touch another frame of film, we cry rape, call them Philistine muck and then throw a brick at anything that moves!"

Coattails flying, he tears out of the room with video cassettes of the show, ready to do battle with the brass. I run after him and catch him at the elevator. What happens, I ask, if they don't run the show in *SNL*'s March 3rd time slot (see Random Notes RS #286), as he hopes?

"Well," he says, now surprisingly calm, "I've always got my poetry, and Gilda is recording one of my songs, 'Let's Talk Dirty to the Animals'—Up yours, Mr. Hippo, piss off, Mr. Fox—on her forthcoming album. If we can't sell the show to cable TV, I guess it'll just have to be a cult cassette."

That week, in the TV Column of the *Washington Post*, NBC vice president Herminio Traviesas is quoted as vowing that *Mondo Video* will only hit the air "over my dead body." The network later denies that Traviesas ever said such a thing, issuing the following statement: "NBC has no air date at this time to present *Mr. Mike's Mondo Video*. The show has not been given an air date due to broadcast standards problems."

At present, O'Donoghue and mentor Lorne Michaels are fighting NBC tooth and nail to run a slightly toned-down version. Barring that, it may be sold to cable TV, the movies, or be or cut up into palatable segments—a tragedy, in my opinion—and aired, at intervals, on *SNL*.

Meanwhile, Michael is in final negotiations with Paramount Pictures to write and direct three of his own films, while his script for a sci-fi epic called *Planet of the Cheap Special Effects*, has been bought by United Artists.

"Michael, you're the Woody Allen of the Eighties!" his agent told him during negotiations with the film studios. There was a long pause. "Does that mean," Michael replied, "that I have to wait another year?"

IS AMERICA READY FOR A PIECE of business like Michael O'Donoghue? That may depend on his ability to prepare us for his hardsell technique. Among his past and present colleagues, loyalists tout him as an artist with total integrity, a man who cannot and will not be compromised. While his detractors view him as a galloping comic ego who prefers the roles of victim and tormentor to those of communicator. Perhaps the real problem is: can Michael strike a truce with humanity long enough to win a few more allies? He confesses with a low laugh that his favorite oneliner is, "Laugh, you assholes!" But one wonders if, in the end, we should be taken in by all this sardonic patter. Is Michael O'Donoghue really humor's answer to Dirty Harry or is there, deep (deep) inside, a trace of tenderness, a *shred* of decency? Well, judge for yourself.

"I want to end up like Oscar Levant!" he cracked disparagingly near the close of our first encounter at his home. "I want to end up a terrible actor with a lovely tremor of the hands, shaking to where I can hardly get the cork-tipped cigarette up to the crooked old mouth. I've already got a silk dressing gown like his and I *hope* you noticed the blood stains on it. If I keep on popping pills I hope to be found floating dead in the pool one day; hopefully one where I can see the bottom.

"Art is such a hard way to go, isn't it? Did you hear about Richard Speck? Paints in the slammer every day, rain or shine. He's a helluva still life artist now, but then I guess he can't be a *landscape* artist, can he? Had to settle for a lot of grey on grey. It's real sad, huh?"

Grim-faced, he leads me to the door, shrugs his shoulders heavily and then extends his hand in fellowship.

"Success, comedy, all these things are great," he tells me. "But what I care about most is my haiku and my work with the little deaf kids on Sundays."

Touched, I grip his hand and gaze deep into his seaweed circles. "One more thing," he entreats, moving closer to murmur in my ear. "Jeane Dixon called me the other day . . . and she said, 'Mike, I predict that without you there on the air, *Supertrain* and Fred Silverman are gonna go right down the dumper!' "

SOME Hosts

HANDTINTED PHOTOGRAPHS BY EDIE BASKIN

Overleaf: Sissy Spacek; Opposite: Art Garfunkel; This page: Jill Clayburgh and Elliott Gould.

This page: Frank Zappa and Robert Klein; Opposite: The Rolling Stones and Cicely Tyson.

This page: Steve Martin and Jodie Foster; Opposite: Walter Matthau.

Opposite: Buck Henry; This page: Candice Bergen, Ralph Nader and Eric Idle.

This page: Louise Lasser and Ron Nessen; Opposite: Paul Simon.

This page: Richard Pryor and Milton Berle; Opposite: Lily Tomlin.

This page: Ray Charles, Rick Nelson and Mary Kay Place; Opposite: Norman Lear.

EDIE BASKIN

LORNE
Michaels

Left, Lorne with music director Howard Shore; below, offering a $3000 check to the Beatles to appear together on the show (they could, he said, split it up any way they wanted to).

EDIE BASKIN

AN
Interview
WITH LORNE MICHAELS

BY TIMOTHY WHITE

IT MIGHT BE FAIR TO SAY THAT the first installment of *Saturday Night Live* was the original casting auditions videotaped on September 9th, 1975. Producer Lorne Michaels screened the hour-long tape of the proceedings for me in his Rockefeller Center offices in the spring of 1979. And I sat watching the now familiar actors take their places, in turn, before the camera, seating themselves in an empty sound booth and nervously fielding improv suggestions, comments and directives.

Dan Aykroyd ambled in to the booth wearing a natty blue blazer, mustache and long sideburns, and he came equipped with a half-dozen characters, among them a Louisiana crab fisherman who'd been abducted by a UFO, a French Canadian lumberjack, a smooth-talking TV salesman for Lloyd Manganero Deltoid Spray ("made from the extracted liquid from the spleens of perfumed sheep"), and a tentative Tom Synder.

Laraine Newman, looking strikingly shapely and healthful, followed Dan with a monologue by Sherri the Stewardess, Laraine's straight, reddish-brown hair hidden under a blonde Sandra Dee wig. An eager-to-please Bill Murray did a creditable impersonation of Duane Thomas, followed by his own characters: oily disc jockey Mel Brewer, a singing cocktail pianist named Bob, and pushy TV personality Jerry Eldini. Chevy Chase looked tense as he winked at the camera. Long-haired John Belushi was relaxed and cocky as he did his Brando bit and some eyebrow exercises. Garrett Morris was sweating heavily, Jane Curtin seemed poised but intimidated, and Andy Kaufman blew his big chance with his eerie recitation of the lyrics to the song, "MacArthur Park." A jumpy, giggling Gilda Radner was too rattled to do anything at all and seemed to sum up everyone's expectations when she said, "Thanks. Can I go now? Back to Toronto?"

There was another voice on the tape, coming from off-camera. It was the calm, tranquilizing sound of Lorne Michaels, cajoling this motley crew into impressing him with that intangible double-shot of television smarts he likes to call "the goods." It was obvious to the camera and to Michaels that virtually all of them had what it takes. It merely remained for *them* to be convinced.

How a nice guy like Toronto-born Lorne Michaels, 34, managed that feat is still a mystery to many. A cautious, reticent man around strangers, he has rarely spoken at length about his phenomenally successful creation and his relationships with his celebrated colleagues. He is known in the industry as a workhorse, a firm, unflappable taskmaster, and a softhearted obses-

sive who admittedly cannot bear to fire anyone in his employ. Certainly, he has done an exceptional job at juggling the fragile and/or volatile egos of the most talented company of comedians on the American scene in the last decade. And if he were to retire at this stage of his career, he would be remembered as the man who brought a unique vitality to a largely stagnant medium.

His accomplishments are obvious, but his nature and techniques remain obscure. In a series of interviews conducted at his Manhattan home and office during May of 1979, Michaels finally talked at length about himself and his work.

Television had become this cold, vacuous, manipulative medium. One night of programming seemed as stale as the next. Then you came along in 1975 with a canny, comedy-oriented show that had a warm likeable company and all the headaches of live television. It was a gallant gesture, but you must be a little nuts to have attempted it. Whenever I think of the potential hazards, I remember the time you booked, or thought you had booked, the Sex Pistols on the show.

Hmmm. I know what you mean. Malcolm McLaren, their manager, contacted us after, I think, seeing Eric Idle host the show. McLaren was in town from London in November of 1977 and he came up to NBC to see me. At the time I was running the finals of the "Anyone Can Host *Saturday Night Live* Contest," and the voting was heavily in favor of Miskell Spellman, the 80-year-old grandmother. McLaren and the band thought that the show that would be hosted by Miskell, in December, would be just perfect for them, so we set a date.

Now, we rarely book anybody very far in advance, certainly no more than a few weeks or so. And the only thing we try to live up to in terms of booking guests is to be accurate in *TV Guide*, whose deadline is ten days before our air date. We kept reconfirming the booking and I told Malcolm that the Pistols were notorious for not showing up, so please keep us posted. But I see in retrospect that it was like asking a mugger not to shoot you—does a lotta good, you know?

They backed out with less than a week to go because, as I understand it, a club in London that the band had been barred from, was suddenly open to them, and they went for the money they could make there. I mean, we can only pay scale. So some harsh words were exchanged, and we called Elvis Costello and he came on and did the show instead.

I heard you were quite upset when Elvis suddenly stopped at the beginning of his second number and began playing another song.

Yeah, it was a rough week, but the wonderful part was that he seized his moment. We always let the musical acts pick their own songs to play. But we spend a lot of time on rehearsals for the show, we block out every camera shot, go through a lot of preparation, so we have to know the music beforehand and time it out exactly 'cause every second counts. So on the second tune, Elvis does a few bars, then suddenly stops. And my heart stopped. I thought, "Here it is, a TV highjacking. He's gonna sing, 'Kill all the niggers, kill all the Jews!'" Or some other apt punk statement. I was stunned, but then I smiled 'cause I knew I wouldn't have to take the heat, and anyway there it was in front of me—*live television*.

But then when he simply began playing another song from his album it was almost anti-climactic.

Viewers wonder about the guests who got away, the hosts who can't or don't sign for the show. Do you have a long list of favored prospects?

That's a question I've managed to duck for four years. I sure would have liked to have had Alec Guinness, Michael Caine or John Cleese host, and maybe I will yet. At one point I

would have loved to have Johnny Carson on. Carson should have done it two years ago; he would have been great at it. I've called him twice and he's been very polite, almost affectionate, but always said no thanks for now. Another person who's always said no is Woody Allen. I wanted to have Billy Martin on after he got fired from the Yankees. He said yes but then backed out.

The guests that work the best are those that can roll with it, and that's not easy. We can't doctor their spots, we can't edit out their mistakes, and a lot of professionals are scared to take that kind of gamble. They feel so vulnerable.

Do you feel vulnerable right now?

Yes. I am uncomfortable with and yet continually seduced into talking about myself. Seduced in the sense that once it starts I start to enjoy it. But it seems to me that the backbone of *Saturday Night,* and what distinguishes it from anything else, are the writers. They are what the show is about—and unfortunately they *now* know it.

In reading magazines like the *New Yorker* or even *Rolling Stone,* you could always tell who wrote what. Or you could look forward to a piece by so and so. I had hoped it would be that way with us. And I think the more discerning viewers of *Saturday Night* now *can* spot a piece by Franken and Davis or a piece by Anne Beatts or by Rosie Shuster or a piece by Alan Zweibel or Tom Schiller, Jim Downey or Herb Sargent.

I don't mean just to list them off 'cause I prefer that they appear not as a crawl. But that has been the most exciting part of the show because they're the people that I'm with the most. The people who have become famous from *Saturday Night Live* have been those performers who are most closely tied to the writing. In this sense, Chevy, to start with, worked as a writer, piously—he worked round the clock. He not only worked for himself, and he *certainly* did that, but he wrote for others as well. He was in there sixteen, eighteen hours a day working. It sounds so Andy Hardy to deal with all this but there is a correlation between effort and reward. You may not get the reward until later or you may get it as in some cases way too soon. Danny, in the same way was there 'round the clock for three years, although less so this year because of his movie commitments. Gilda still is, Billy is, Laraine is. Jane, not as much. Garrett, in and out, depending upon how he feels. John, in the very first year was there all the time. There wouldn't be a Samurai without him going over all of the props. I remember the first Samurai he did, he brought a picture of Toshiro Mifune into makeup. He was so precise, he cared so much.

When you say being there all the time, what do you mean?

When I was first putting together the schedule of work, it came out to nine days. That was the luxurious schedule. I cut it down to seven days, and then we only had six. Even so, in the six days all things happen simultaneously. As the script is being written, the sets are being designed. A film is being shot. All of it is happening and it's always problem solving at a rate that's out of control.

Give me an example of the nuts and bolts of this process.

No matter how good or bad the show's been the Saturday night before, on the following Monday there's no show. I go in during the early or late afternoon because Monday morning is my morning of rest. There will generally be an earlier meeting between myself and whoever the host is that week. If I haven't met the person before, I try to get a sense of whether or not they can do the show or try to explain it to them.

Because the show is not done on tape I can't say, "When we have the music and the laugh

track, the mistakes won't show," or whatever. I can only say that I'll try and it could be the most humiliating night of your life. Those who are brave enough to, come along anyway. Candy Bergen once compared it to being kidnapped.

You're suddenly in an environment in which you are the focus that week–but that's assuming Belushi comes out of his dressing room.

Then there will be a writer's meeting, a meeting in which all of the writers will come in and try and convince me or the host that they've actually given some thought to that week's show.

Is there much of a carryover from the previous show, from sketches that didn't get on?

Yes, quite often. For example, last week there was a sketch that Jim Downey wrote about Idi Amin staying with a couple. A normal, young suburban couple. There's no real reason given why he's staying there, but it's a thing of getting rid of somebody who's staying in your apartment for weeks, only in his case there's an antelope carcass in the kitchen that he's neglected to clean up, and victims of torture in the closet. The piece was very funny and certainly ready to go on last week but we were 29 minutes long at dress and it could be held.

On a Monday I begin to get a sense of the shape of the show, just the barest sense of it. And the hosts generally get terrified. They tend to lose heart at that meeting because the ideas then are in very raw form, but as I continually point out, if the writers could talk they wouldn't be writers. Generally people have freedom to present any idea that they want and also the freedom to go write it if they believe in it. I have to listen on about five or ten levels: Is it achievable? Can a set be built? How do you present it? What cast members does it involve? How much time is it during the show? What end of the studio will it be set up in? There's a finite space for design. And what director Dave Wilson and I try and do, to use a clumsy metaphor, is find enough colors to make a rainbow. And hopefully, it isn't a black rainbow.

Last spring the show had a sketch in dress rehearsal with the central character of arch-villain Dr. V. Neck. Danny is a James Bond-type secret agent out to stop him. Everybody was involved in it, and there were four elaborate sets and it was never seen or heard from again.

It's actually been seen again but only at dress rehearsals. It never went stale, we just never found an ending to it. It had one of my favorite jokes in it. Jim Downey wrote a joke in which Bond is being shown a new elaborate piece of luggage. The man says, "The boys in lab came up with this suitcase, and your shirts go over here, your toiletries go here in the plastic container with the zipper...."

I remember Gilda telling me at one point last summer that you sometimes encourage people to take things from their personal lives and use them on the show. John's "Don't Look Back in Anger" sketch involving Chevy got on the air.

Yes, what John was going through at the time was revealed on the show. I even did one with Chevy two weeks after he'd left the show on the Paul Simon Thanksgiving show where Paul came out dressed as a turkey. He was on his way to the studio and Chevy was outside playing a guitar and people were throwing change in the guitar case. And Chevy was certainly good enough to go along with it at the time....

You seem to give the players a lot of rope.

Chevy doing Ford the first time was, hey, what do we need, let's get a podium in, we're going to do the president! In most of the cases when Chevy used to do falls, they were never thought of until that moment. I like to keep the "backstage" part of the show alive.

What began to happen I think more last year and this year is that people like John suddenly had a whole public image and became more aware of not wanting to be seen in a bad light. So they had a lot more to lose—or John felt he had a lot more to lose in being portrayed as somebody who did drugs.

There was a piece once that Al Franken wrote, based on an idea of Michael O'Donoghue's, that the network decided that the name Belushi could not make it; they thought it was too ethnic, and therefore convinced him to change his name to Kevin Scott. It made me laugh a lot, and we were going to the point of having Kevin Scott in the opening montage, under John's picture. But John didn't like it because he felt in some way it made fun of the name Belushi. I didn't see that but I had to respect that sensitivity on his part.

The show became a powerful vehicle for exposure and overexposure.

Many of the cast members were on covers of magazines and being bombarded when they went outside. So that privacy becomes real important. In the first year we did a cold opening once where Buck Henry couldn't get into the studio, because the guard didn't know who he was. And I had to come down and get him. That was based on a reality. It wasn't Buck who it happened to, it had been Elliott Gould.

I used to do that all the time, responding to whatever was happening. I would tend to want to keep the show fresh and completely topical so if a political announcement like the State of the Union address came on Thursday, we would do it on Saturday. I think at our best, people look forward to us hitting or going after whatever the big story of that week was. So when Three Mile Island happened, we *had* to do the Pepsi Syndrome that week. So in those situations, I pull out the stops. The show tends to go over budget those weeks because I tend

Left, Lorne in rehearsal with Tony Perkins & Jane; below, director Dave Wilson; opposite, the SNL band dressed to the Tut, playing backup for Steve Martin.

to go crazy in wanting to respond because I think that the audience is forever grateful—forever in television being about six months.

Do you have a philosophy about the importance of accuracy in comedy, and in television entertainment?

Well I always felt that the show at its best was a record of what had gone on that week in the country, the world, and in the lives of the people doing the show. Sincerity had been devalued in modern American show business to the point where somebody on television would say "my very very best friend" to some guest who they had been introduced to about twenty minutes before by two William Morris agents. If you watch the good-nights on *SNL* carefully you can see how the hosts and the cast relate to each other. I don't mean just hugging and kissing or any of that shit. You can tell that there's been, say, tension, or whatever.

In retrospect, speaking of things taken from the cast members' personal lives, the things that I thought were best were the "Judy Miller" things. Anybody could appreciate them.

EDIE BASKIN

I was a fan of the "Judy Miller Show" and I felt it was one of the best collaborations between Marilyn Miller and Gilda.

It was Gilda and Marilyn sharing their childhood experiences with the audience.

Absolutely. Just like Marilyn's "Slumber Party," or Todd and Lisa, the nerds, which Rosie and Anne wrote. Those are the kinds of things I tend to be proudest of. It's now gotten to the point where those pieces get an ovation for just showing up. But the style of the show has been to kill off its successful things. Just so that one remembers that the person's name is Gilda Radner, *not* Emily Litella or Roseanne Roseanadanna.

Will most of the popular characters endure?

Some will. I remember the biggest fear that I had when Chevy was leaving the show—'cause we were doing the debates between Ford and Carter—was that Ford might win. I knew I had Carter in Danny, but Chevy's Ford was leaving the show. Somebody is going to have to learn to do Jerry Brown soon.

Danny's so amazing he's weird....

And he never, ever breaks character. It's a distinction that is often made with John and Danny. I remember seeing the Blues Brothers for the first time and they came out and they were both perfectly in character as Jake and Elwood. But Danny more I think—Danny *becomes* Elwood totally. The Nazis could get hold of Danny and he wouldn't break character. He may tell them where the tanks are but he would do it in character. At the L.A. concert, John said, "Hello from New York." It was sweet and it acknowledged the audience and it was a personal hello, but *Jake* wouldn't have said it in a million years, 'cause Jake's from Joliet, Illinois.

I know that the record companies feel that SNL can sell a lot of records for an act.

Oh sure. But at a certain period in the Sixties performers would turn their backs to their audience and play to their amps which I always found to be a less-than-moving experience. And it seemed as if the brand of show business that I wanted to be part of was over. It belonged to Milton Berle or to some relics from the past; it was in a museum someplace. Not that I love the excesses of that kind of show business, its false notes, but there was something very honest in the direct presentation of coming out and facing the audience. And people like Lenny Bruce or Richard Pryor or Steve Martin for that matter, carried it on, representing us and articulating for us. *SNL* does that now, probably better than anything else on television, in my opinion, with the possible exception of *Sixty Minutes.*

What single thing on television have you seen, as an adult, that deeply moved you? A show, a moment?

I remember when I was fairly lonely and bottomed out at a certain time. I remember watching a *Mary Tyler Moore* show and crying.

What happened on the show?

Nothing. It was just a particularly good episode and it had to do with the friendship between her and Rhoda. But I don't want to be remembered as the guy who cried at the *Mary Tyler Moore Show.* When I've been working too hard and haven't had a chance to feel anything because I've lived in my brain for too long, then I can be touched or moved by something, not necessarily sentimental, but

something sweet or tender or any kind of generosity.

What I'm talking about is, not TV so much as the entertainment part of it. I can remember being enormously moved when my brother was in Vietnam and I saw a soldier get seriously injured on the evening news films. Also, a woman whose family had just died in a fire out in Brooklyn. And I was moved in both cases. Life is so frail. TV was reminding me what real life is like, and that's a strange experience.

And the American tradition that I most identify with and loved as a kid was the one where we know how overwhelmingly sad and mean life is, and so we tend to deal with it with humor. So you get the hard-boiled reporter, you get the people who develop an edge in order to protect themselves against the very things you're talking about.

I as a Canadian, and probably more as an immigrant, took Watergate real seriously in terms of truth, justice and the American way. I was outraged, shocked; the child in me was shocked and so was the adult. I felt Nixon had to go to jail if everyone else was going to jail. And if some guy can be hung or shot for taking a couple of bucks from the gas station or 7-11, surely bombing Cambodia deserves something.

You said you were writing a lot of anti-Nixon stuff during your one season (1968-69) as a "Laugh-In" writer.

Well it's the God-given right of Canadians to fuck with American politics. And since a good deal of Canada is dominated certainly by American culture and American industry and we have what is sometimes referred to as a branch-plant economy, you just grow up fascinated by America. We got American television before we got Canadian television. CBC didn't start broadcasting until the mid-Fifties, I think. By the time Canada television got on I was kind of hooked on American television. Except if you watched *Howdy Doody* and they advertised Snickers you got to see *"Not Available in Canada"* superimposed at the end of the commercial.

As a boy, what was your home life like?

My dad was a furrier. And then he got out of that and went into a kind of semi-retirement. But my grandparents owned a movie house, the College Playhouse, on College Street in Toronto. My mother worked in the box office, my uncle was a projectionist, my grandmother would police the place and was a kind of bouncer. So from the time I was three or four years of age, I remember being babysat in the theater. I think I was carried screaming from the theater at age 4 after seeing the *Wizard of Oz.*

Why did your father go into semi-retirement? Was he ill?

I think he just had it. He was a man who was the responsible one in the family. I think he was the person who took care of others. He reached a certain point in his life, he married late, where his former responsibilities were behind him. He died when I was fourteen. He was 48. Dying young is a family tradition.

The point I wanted to make about my grandparents and my aunts and my mother in particular was that dinner table conversation could easily be about Humphrey Bogart or Clark Gable or Spencer Tracey. My grandmother talked about those people very much like they were friends of the family. If she didn't like W.C. Fields—and she didn't because she believed he was anti-Semitic—she didn't play his picture. It was a small family business on what was College Street, right by the University of Toronto. I cowrote and directed a show at UC in 1964 which was very successful.

Then Hart Pomerantz and I wrote a lot of things for CBC radio, various things, all the things that you do to make a living or to just

get by. We wrote the Canadian Army show, and a General Motors industrial show. Eventually we went to work on CBC-Radio's *The Russ Thompson Show,* which was 90 minutes, five days a week, and based on *The Tonight Show.* Hart and I performed once a week on it live. Stand-up for radio, with a live audience. We were kind of a hit in a modest way.

What was the gist of your shtick?

We would do an interview with an airline pilot with a bad memory. Nowhere near Rowan and Martin but in the style of two-man comedy. I was the straight man. Hart and I were later to get a fifteen-minute show Wednesday nights at 10 o'clock which was a satirical show on CBC radio called *Five Nights a Week at this Time.* From there we began to write monologues and perform which led to some coming down to New York which led to working with Woody which led to working with Joan Rivers.

How did you meet Woody Allen?

Hart met Woody I think. I'm trying to think of how that all came about. I would like to get the sequence right for you. I think it was through Jack Rollins, Woody's manager, a wonderful man.

Was Woody still doing any stand-up then?

Yes, he was. It was pre-*Take the Money and Run.* He was the first person that I ever wrote for and I don't think that I added a joke to his life or anything. At the time Woody was doing jokes like smoking a joint and trying to give the Statue of Liberty a hickey. He then read the monologue and we had our first meeting with him and he explained something that I still remember vividly: He said that *he* is his premise. The premises don't have to be silly: he did the same jokes as Bob Hope. This was a giant leap for me. I remember Hart and I going to the Russian Tea Room after and having a big argument because Hart couldn't understand or didn't want to understand that Woody does the same jokes as Bob Hope, because Bob Hope was clearly so different. And I think I was more sympathetic to Woody's point. I was much more drawn to writing than Hart was. That was eventually the conflict that broke us up.

At the time I remember I wrote a silly joke. I can't remember the exact set-up, but it had to do with being obsessed with the fact that you could not have a original thought because whatever thought you were thinking, somewhere else there was probably someone else in the world also thinking that at the same time. And it was a sequence of tracking that person down. But everytime you called—the line was busy! And it was in that kind of over-intellectual, over-convoluted structure. But Woody liked it. I was trying to imitate Woody's style and he was just enormously encouraging. When I came to do *Saturday Night* in 1975, he had a New Year's party that he invited me to, and when he saw me—we hadn't seen each other in nine years, eight years—he said, "You've grown up." It was then that I began to get a perspective of just how young I must have been.

In *Laugh-In* I only learned about politics . . . *The Beautiful Phyllis Diller Show* was an eye-opening experience for me. Her opening line in the first audience warm-up was, "What's brown and has holes in it? Swiss shit." Well, needless to say, after that warm-up it was smooth sailing. "What has hair and hangs from a wall? Humpty Cunt." That was the *second* joke. It went on to four in the morning and there was champagne served on the studio floor afterwards and people were congratulating everyone and Rosie Shuster, who I was then married to, said, "You know it's garbage, don't you?" I didn't. This was the beginning of the realization that I had to pay very close attention.

It always seems easiest to dig a hole deeper.

And it's also like the Vietnamese War—"While we're in it we might as well win it." And that's what happens. There's a morality that takes over in process, and process and structure and determinism, are the things that began to obsess me. I became a producer to protect my writing, which was being fucked over by producers.

So I was in L.A. in 1972 for that summer and did a Burns and Schreiber show for ABC. And at that same time I met Lily Tomlin. A mutual friend of ours, Ann Elder, had seen the shows that I had done in Canada.

If Bob Hope was doing a sketch on marijuana on TV at that time, the people acted like they were drunk. I was outraged. But the Smothers Brothers broke through to some degree; that was a much hipper show than *Laugh-In* was at the time. I was very envious of the people who worked on that show because they were people of my generation who were working in television. *Laugh-In* had that appearance but the writers and the style was very much from another time and another place.

Lily Tomlin looked at my stuff from Canada and asked me to work with her. She also said that if I ever wanted to direct, she saw something that I had directed, that she would help if she could. She was just enormously generous and kind. The first time we met we spent about seven hours together talking. And I criticized her work and she didn't criticize my work, and then I felt badly 'cause she was so much more gracious than I was. But she was probably the formative influence on me and probably changed more about the way I approached comedy than anyone previously. At a point where I had very little self-confidence she said, "I appreciate you and I appreciate your work." And that was an enormous compliment. No one had ever given me anything that had ever meant as much. Woody Allen had called a joke I did brilliant once and that kept me going for four or five years.

I worked with Lily on her first special, *The Lily Show*, which was for CBS which a network official was to call a $360,000 jerk-off. Herb Sargent was the producer of the show. I was a writer on it. Well, the show went on the air in November, 1973, and won an Emmy. I had gotten an Emmy nomination on *Laugh-In* but I felt like I was standing next to the guy who gets shot and you both get the purple heart or whatever. Give me time and I'll work on that metaphor.

How did you pick the cast and format for SNL?

Well, I did not want to say yes to anyone until I had a definite go. But I already knew Danny and Gilda from Toronto and saw John and Bill in *The National Lampoon Show*. I wanted them all. What made the show so successful, I think, were the girls.

You know, I've always had a problem with the *National Lampoon*'s humor. I guess the phrase "jock" covers it. There was a kind of male-ego sweat-socks attitude in it, which I never have really been a part of. I have to admit I have a certain anger towards the magazine. This guy Matty Simmons who owns the *National Lampoon* has come after the show and has attacked me several times in print, saying I discovered Gilda and John and Bill in *The National Lampoon Show* and then lifted a lot of ideas and other nonsense. I certainly see Michael O'Donoghue's influence on the show. And he, of course, was a former *Lampoon* editor. His influence, particularly at the beginning, was enormous but I always thought Second City had more of an influence on the show, because so many of the cast members had been trained in improvisation. For three years I taught improvisation in Toronto at the New School of Art. And when Hart and I performed, we always worked with improvisation. It seemed like that was much more the tradition of the show than any specific literary tradition.

Franken and Davis—I read a piece of their material before I hired them. They were the only people I didn't meet first. They just arrived, they were from Minneapolis and had been working out of L.A. They had never written for television before, but their material was on the paper. They were the only people that I hired that way. Chevy came out of a sense of talking with him, Michael that way, Anne that way. I never read anything Anne or Michael wrote till after I hired them. Laraine had worked with Lily and me, and Jane auditioned. Garrett was recommended to me.

John did the Samurai at the audition, didn't he?

Yes. Chevy actually was urging me to hire John. And Chevy was a writer at that point, not a cast member. John and I have a kind of grudging respect and affection for one another.

Tell me about the first time you met him.

Belushi came in for a meeting with me and he was heavily bearded at the time. And he had this stance of his—he was a radical actor, he wasn't going to do television. And I said, "Thank you very much, that's fine. Why are you here?" Well, he heard that I represented something new in television. But the more that he would talk about how television was shit, the more that I would say that I loved television. He only made me harden my position. It's been the story of our relationship. I'm continually making him harden his position. And someday we'll get married.

Is the story true about you sitting in the barber's chair at Danny's 505 Club in Toronto, talking about what kind of show it was going to be and all that?

I've been to the 505 Club. There was never a moment's doubt in my mind that Dan Aykroyd would be on the show. There was, however, apprehension. If you saw the expression on Michael O'Donoghue's face and Chevy

Chase's face the day Dan Aykroyd first came to the office . . . I believe the phrase Michael used was "rough trade." Michael was terrified of Dan. He hated him because he was a total threat to Michael's prissiness. Michael had no eyes for those kinds of people but he loves Danny now.

But I didn't know quite what the show was going to be. The first thing that I did when I agreed to do it was, Tom Schiller—who was then my assistant, later to be a writer and filmmaker on the show—and I went to Joshua Tree, which is a place outside of Los Angeles in the desert. This was in June of '75. And I just sat there and just thought a lot. And formatted it and conceptualized it and realized that this was the kind of show that I wanted.

I recall someone saying that you two took acid.

You heard those stories? I was doing a lot of mushrooms at that time. Yes, there were some psychedelics ingested. But you're relating the two things as if it all happened in some sort of vision.

Oh no I'm not. All I'm asking is what you did. How long were you out there for?

I don't recall actually. It might have been months. That was probably because of the drugs. What happened was we talked and talked and Tom is wonderfully funny. I came back and I knew the format I wanted.

It was scary. I talked to NBC a lot about finding the show on the air and that with comedy shows it was necessary to see what to emphasize, where the hit was, as it were. I think the brass at NBC were real open to it. Television executives are not morons. They are generally bright people who are caught in an economic system that demands a certain kind of meat and potatoes approach. No different than anything else in American industry.

What thought had you given to studio design?

Eugene and Franne Lee, two Broadway designers, saw the studio 8-H and came up with the design, although we've changed it every year for four years. But the balcony was there because I wanted the audience right on top of the cast because with comedy it's real important that there be that eye contact and proximity. And I wanted a stage because stages are important psychologically for performing.

The set looks a little ragged. That's the look I wanted; not terribly slick. It's what New York was at that time and, by and large, still is—deteriorated, run down and loved because of it. It has the feeling of an old shoe. It seems to me that the comedy that I wanted to do needed that kind of *reality.*

You use that word—reality—a lot in describing the show.

I did LSD once and I had this incredibly profound revelation on it which was that things are seldom what they seem. The intensity of the experience is such that you tend to remember it just as if somebody steps out from the shadows, grabs you by the shirt collar and puts a gun to your temple. Things become incredibly lucid.

And the only comparable experience I know of is that the show has to go on. It's a tradition, an old, old, cliche, but in live television it actually *has* to go on. It's either that or a test pattern.

Will nothing be as good as live television? Will you stay in live television?

There was a play years ago on Broadway that I saw called *That Championship Season* which Jason Miller wrote, which I loved quite a good deal. In it there were these five guys and a coach. Nothing ever had as much force or intensity to their lives as that one period of their lives. You can put off dealing with your entire life by working that hard. I think that I'm compulsive.

I would like to do a movie and probably *will*, but I'm less interested in doing in movies what I've already done in television. I wouldn't have wanted to do *Animal House*. I was not a fraternity guy. I'm from the decade called the Sixties which was in reaction to all of that and I didn't like any of the values, the elitism, of fraternities.

Do you think that the pressures of doing a live show like SNL have a destructive quality to them?

Yes. There have been a lot of breakdowns on the show, in all aspects of the staff. No one can withstand the pressure of that show. The odd part is that you can see everybody else going under, you never see yourself going under. But clearly there have been moments when I was doing just that.

What was the hardest single time for you?

It was a very difficult time right after Chevy left because I was not prepared for it. In the first place, I didn't think it would happen and also I had only thought the show through that first season. I had a strong belief of how to make it a hit, how to get it to that point, but I didn't know anything about maintaining anything. Chevy had been the focus of a lot of the show. John fell apart right after Chevy left. I think because John felt that he was neglected on the show and was not getting the attention he felt he should from the press. Then suddenly Chevy was gone and the burden of leadership fell to John. He just collapsed under it, he just went away. So there was the problem of having to pull him through a very difficult period, an incredibly self-destructive period. Meanwhile I had to get the show together and at the same time I was going through self-doubt myself. Danny once, in an argument that we had, screamed at me, "We've done it! I don't know why we have to keep doing it!" I had no answer then. I think I have one now: *because it's what we do.*

But what does SNL mean to you?

SNL, I wanted it to be devoid of definition, much the way I wanted my life to be. I didn't want it to be a comedy show, a political show, I didn't want it to be a musical show, the mandate was to be experimental. Whenever it was getting to the point where smugness was about to creep in, I tried to kick it around a little. The hardest part was that it was a secret that the world found out about. So if a movie studio was telling John Belushi that he was the biggest star in the world and he was on the cover of *Newsweek,* it was impossible to say to him, 'John, you've gotta push it, you've gotta try something new here or you're going to be yesterday's news.' Because the pressure for him was to do Samurai, to stick with the hit.

In my heart of hearts I truly believe that the people at NBC do not know what they have here. No more than RCA knew what they had when they had Elvis Presley on the disc years ago.

What's supposed to happen? Is the show going on for another few years?

It's going on. As far as NBC is concerned it's going on for another 20 years. But as far as I'm concerned it's one week at a time.

Do you think, in retrospect, that it was a mistake for Chevy to leave?

An enormous mistake for him to leave. But I think that doesn't need to be said anymore, I think everybody understands that. Not in terms of success or failure. But just on the level that there was so much more that he could have done on the show. The show challenged Chevy to keep taking risks. He had to go on half the time on "Update" with very thin material sometimes because everybody was too burnt out to get to it or whatever and he made it shine.

But everybody else had signed for five years. I had only signed for three years. Suddenly at the middle of last year, I told everybody that I was leaving when my contract was up. It didn't dawn on me that *SNL* is what I do, or this is what makes me happy. You begin to think that, "Jesus I'm an asshole for still being here. So-and-so signed with Universal, so-and-so signed with Paramount." But the quickest way to kill off somebody talented is to let them do everything that they want.

Still, it's inevitable that the best of repertory companies break up.

People leave the show but no one can be replaced. I didn't try and look for a tall guy who falls when Chevy left. I went for someone else who I thought was very talented.

Television is not an art. If it is, forgive me for using it. You can go into a room and write a screenplay or a novel and you don't need anyone else. In television there are hundreds of pairs of hands that get in the way of it or help it along.

In our first conversation you were talking about how you have faith in TV and think it's worthwhile.

I'm real proud of it—but only when it's done right.

I think of television as a medium filled with blown opportunities, and a lot of people would not want to see talents like Don Hewitt of "60 Minutes" and yourself leave television. It happens too often and the industry is left with a lot of morons out in Burbank writing "Charlie's Angels."

Maybe it's just too difficult to do a good job. But I'm in a completely unique position now in late-night. There really is no competition against *SNL*. And the show has been there longer than any of the executives who are now there, so the show has seniority in a sense. I don't think it will be tampered with.

I love the passion with which certain people work for and care about the show. And then there are those who just give interviews about how much they care. I'm sorry that this bitterness keeps coming out. Dick Ebersol has this theory of the solitary passionate man, in that almost all things that get done get done because one person will not give up. But I think that there are many, many people that are passionate about what they do, and they often form extremely productive groups.

In either case, I think that obsession is a virtue.

But the pressure to give them less is so great in television because the traffic will bear almost anything. I think if I were the Fonz or if I were Chico, or Mork for that matter, well, I think it's going to be real hard to be Mork in about *two* years. I like diversity, I like the anonymity that I had up until we spoke.

What do you think you've contributed?

A chunk of my intestines and a large part of my brain. There is a credit in television called "created by" which I don't take because I always think that no one person does. But I certainly was present at the birth. And I feel this loyalty, it's hard to describe. Loving the show is like loving humanity and yet not liking people. There's this thing called the *SNL* show that is greater than any of the stars on it, and greater than any of the writers or the network that it's on, in the sense that it *must* have its own integrity. Occasionally if a writer is in a slump I have been known to put a piece on that isn't as good as usual so that person will have the confidence to attack the page again. But beyond that, I fight for the show itself.

You seem determined, and yet very wistful.

We were off at Christmas [of 1978] and I was on an island in the Caribbean that I don't want anyone to know about and I was walking on the beach with Howard Shore. Howard and I have known each other since high school, and he's musical director on the show. We were walking along, and he said, "Are you gonna do it again?" And I said, "Howard, I don't know." But Howard said, "It's too bad because we're just learning how to do it."

Such is the arrogance of winning too many awards too early. We moved television ahead about a quarter of an inch and there's dancing in the streets. I think the season that it is not better than the last one will be when I get out. And I will probably stay on too long as all people in comedy ultimately do. But I hope that I'll know. The only thing that could fuck it up now is what fucks up *everything*—success.

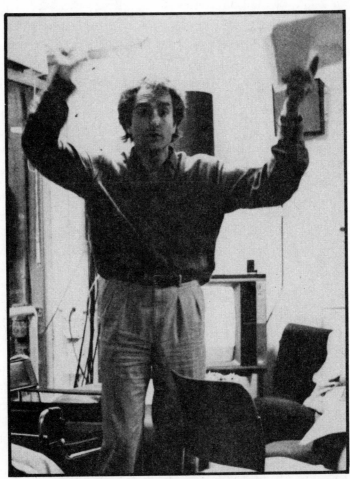

JEAN C. PIGOZZI